# GRAND TIMES IN
# Grand Rapids

# Grand Times in Grand Rapids

## Pieces of Furniture City History

Gordon G. Beld

Foreword by Tom Rademacher

The History Press

Published by The History Press
Charleston, SC 29403
www.historypress.net


*Opposite page*: After starting his career as a part-time custodian at the Grand Rapids plant of Leonard Refrigerator Company, George H. Beld moved up the corporate ladder and became its manager after consolidation with American Motors Corporation.

First published 2012

Published in cooperation with Gemini Publications, publisher of *Grand Rapids Magazine*. Most of the stories in this book were first printed within its pages.

Manufactured in the United States
ISBN 978.1.60949.629.6

Beld, Gordon, 1927-
Grand times in Grand Rapids : pieces of Furniture City history / Gordon Beld.
p. cm.
"Published in cooperation with Gemini Publications, publisher of Grand Rapids magazine, in which most of the stories in this book were first printed."
Includes index.
ISBN 978-1-60949-629-6
1. Grand Rapids (Mich.)--History--Anecdotes. 2. Grand Rapids (Mich.)--Social life and customs--Anecdotes. 3. Grand Rapids (Mich.)--Biography--Anecdotes. I. Gemini Publications (Firm) II. Grand Rapids magazine. III. Title.
F574.G7B37 2012
977.4'56--dc23
2012007678

*For*
*the most amazing man I've ever known, my father, George H. Beld,*
*and my mother, Josephine (De Young) Beld,*
*whose devotion to the happiness and success*
*of her husband and children was equally amazing.*

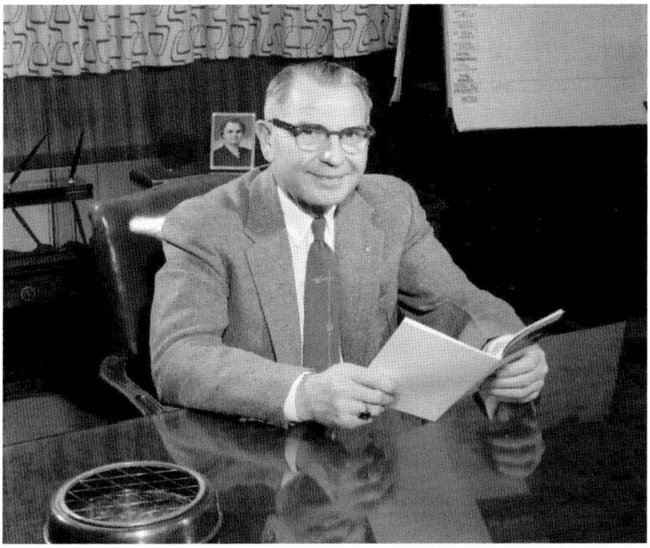

*They met when they were students at Godfrey School, just outside the southwest city limits of Grand Rapids. During his days there, Dad worked part time as a floor sweeper at Leonard Refrigerator Company. He was sixteen when he graduated from the tenth grade in 1919, and he took a few courses at a local business college before ending his formal education and starting full-time work at Leonard as an accountant. Through the years, his employer's name changed to Grand Rapids Refrigerator Company, Kelvinator, Nash-Kelvinator and then American Motors. His positions changed to manager of cost and payroll department, assistant chief inspector, personnel director, production manager, assistant plant manager and finally plant manager. As plant manager during the last ten years of his career of more than forty-five years with the company, he worked closely with George W. Romney, American Motors president and, later, governor of Michigan.*

# Contents

# Foreword

You only have to meet Gordon Beld once.

Maybe it's the way he gently trains his eyes on you and asks something beyond casual. It could be the manner in which he gets to the point—succinctly, yet with grace. Or perhaps it's just his disarming demeanor, belying the power with which he writes.

Gordon was a newspaperman long before he started penning historical narratives. Working off and on for more than twenty years at the *Grand Rapids Press* and the now-defunct *Grand Rapids Herald*, Gordon cut his teeth on stories that helped develop an impeccable sense of fairness, an uncanny word economy and the innate ability to differentiate fact from fiction from opinion.

Those are essential hallmarks for any good reporter and are just as vital to anyone entrusted with conveying a true sense of the past. But Gordon brings something else to the table as well: the ability to write with high imagery, transporting you and me to other times and other places.

His passion for refugees also makes him uniquely qualified to write from the heart, acknowledging the visceral ways in which all of us are connected to people and places as well as things of days gone by.

Gordon treats everyone with the same degree of dignity, whether it's Miss Michigan of 1961, the late president Gerald R. Ford or an old-time barnstorming pilot—all subjects in the compelling stories he's sculpted for his audiences.

He has also served as a mentor for more than one up-and-coming writer, myself included. At twenty, I was a kid at Alma College without a clue, thrust into the role of student sports information director without so much as a rough blueprint. More than once, Gordon saved my hide and eventually helped me realize the dignity that accompanied writing well for a living.

This compendium of stories authored by Gordon for *Grand Rapids Magazine* is nothing less than a keepsake. I encourage you to sit back and enjoy a master storyteller as he breathes life into some of the important touchstones that define our rich and varied pasts.

Consider yourselves introduced.

—Tom Rademacher

*A lifelong resident of the Grand Rapids area, Tom Rademacher is a nationally acclaimed newspaper columnist who wrote full time for the* Grand Rapids Press *for more than three decades. During two of the last three years, the National Society of Newspaper Columnists awarded him first place for columns in competition against the largest papers in the United States.*

# Gratitude for Grand People

The Grand Rapids area is noted not only for its grand times but also for its grand people. There are the big names, of course, like President Gerald and Mrs. Betty Ford, Senator Arthur Vandenberg and astronauts Roger Chaffee and Jack Lousma. But there are thousands of other grand folks who didn't make many headlines. They've just made life better for the rest of us. A lot of them opened doors for me and pulled me through them. They're the ones who made it possible for me to spend nearly seventy years doing what I like best: writing. So, before getting into the stories themselves, I'd like to tell you about some of these grand people.

MARTHA SCHUITEMA. As the principal and teacher of the seventh and eighth grades at the five-room Newhall School in suburban Wyoming Township, Mrs. Schuitema was a strict disciplinarian and nobody's favorite teacher. But she taught me all I know about the grammar and mechanics so essential for my life's work.

NEWELL BURT. Mr. Burt was the basketball coach at Wyoming Park High School who, during my junior year, invited me to be his team's manager. Part of the job was serving as scorekeeper, and that prompted me to check out the possibility of writing game reports for one of the local newspapers.

RALPH TRUAX. It was a Saturday morning, February 12, 1944, when a kid with a dream walked into the editorial office of the *Grand Rapids Press* and walked out a professional writer. I was the kid. Ralph, assistant sports editor of the paper, was at his desk when I arrived and asked if I could report my school's games for him. He had me type out two paragraphs

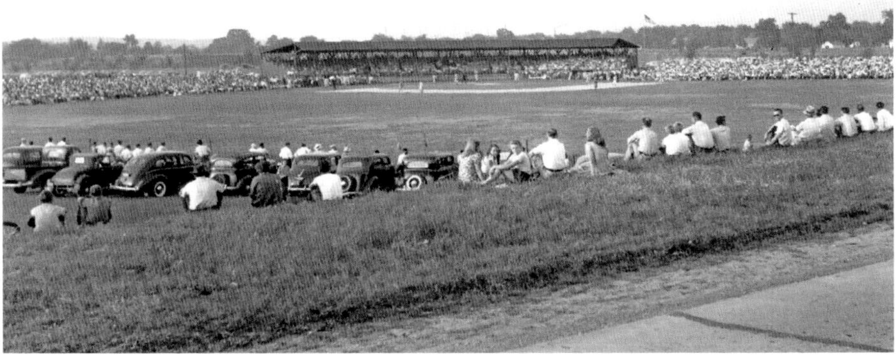

An overflow crowd circled the playing field at Lamar Park in suburban Wyoming Township on August 1, 1944, when the Detroit Tigers took on the West Michigan All-Stars. *Courtesy of Grand Rapids History and Special Collections, Archives, Grand Rapids Public Library.*

about our game of the night before, and when the paper landed on our doorstep that afternoon, there they were—right there on the sports page and completely unchanged. Ralph then provided more opportunities, and soon I was covering all athletic activities of two suburban leagues—a job with a pay rate of three cents per printed line, making me one of the richest kids at Wyoming Park.

Roscoe Bennett. This all-business *Press* sports editor wasn't known to be overly friendly or encouraging, but during the summer of 1944, he sent the paper's sixteen-year-old copy boy (me) out to cover an exhibition game of the Detroit Tigers. At the top of my report in the next day's *Press* was my first-ever byline. Roscoe's kindness provided the biggest thrill I'd experienced up to that time.

Kenneth Davis. Wyoming Park's principal, as well as my geometry and chemistry teacher, Mr. Davis knew that during my lackluster senior year of study, I was learning more at the *Press* than in the classroom. So, on mornings when I'd arrive at school hours late after spending time at the sports desk writing stories of the previous night's games, he'd always cheerfully sign a pass admitting me to class.

Lee Woodruff. When I left for military service in 1946, Mr. Woodruff gave me a "to whom it may concern" letter saying that I'd make a good addition to an army newspaper staff. It didn't impress any of the officers who made assignments, and I was sent to Arkansas for training as a rifleman and then to Germany, where I became a trooper in the Sixty-sixth Squadron of the U.S. Constabulary. When I returned to Grand Rapids after my discharge, Ralph Truax had been reassigned, and I was unable to regain my part-time position on the sports desk. Then Mr. Woodruff offered me a full-time job, but I turned it down so I could complete college studies.

JOHN FLANAGAN. This genial Irishman and assistant sports editor of the *Grand Rapids Herald* welcomed me aboard to write for that paper when I was unable to continue part-time at the *Press*. I wrote for the *Herald* from that year, 1947, until the paper ceased publication in 1959.

CLYDE GEERLINGS. During my days of study at Hope College, Clyde was its director of public relations, and he hired me as a part-time student assistant, handling sports publicity. Working with Clyde was a joy, and it led to my decision that a PR job with a small liberal arts college would be a great way to earn a living. From those days on, my career goal was to do just that.

RUSSELL (RUD) FORMSMA. Three days after receiving my degree from Hope in 1950, the girl of my dreams, Marty Debbink, and I were married in Milwaukee; when we arrived in Grand Rapids after our honeymoon, a call from Rud, superintendent of Kelloggsville Public Schools, offered a teaching job. He was a great administrator, and working with him for a decade was a delight.

ALBERT L. DEAL. As superintendent of Wyoming Public Schools, Al invited me to join his staff and move into educational public relations in the early 1960s. I quickly accepted the offer. A few years earlier, he and Rud had invited me to attend a meeting at which the OK Conference was established by six suburban school districts. Their invitation to the meeting enabled me, then writing for the *Herald* as well as teaching, to scoop the *Press* with the story.

EDWARD F. WIEST. As mayor of the city of Wyoming, Ed enabled me to become involved in historical activities other than teaching and writing when he named me to the city's Historical and Cultural Commission in 1964. I was privileged to become the group's first chairman. Ed was also the owner of an auto parts store that sold Michigan automobile licenses, and he always saved a plate for me that had easy-to-remember numbers.

CHARLES L. CLAPP. During the years he served as managing editor of the *Herald*, he made it possible for me to move beyond sports writing and into general reporting and feature writing. Charlie was a real newspaperman, the kind you used to see in the movies. I think he had printers' ink instead of blood. Though he was persistent in his efforts to get me to leave teaching and to work full time at the paper, I was able to resist. I'm grateful, too, that one of his assignments provided my first opportunity to write local history. It resulted in a page-one story concerning pioneer Grand Rapids aviator Bert Kenyon, and it served as an appetizer for more of that kind of writing.

WERNER VEIT. When the *Herald* was bought out by owners of the *Press* in 1959, several staff members moved next door to help the *Press* establish a Sunday edition. Werner, who had been Charlie's successor as managing editor of the *Herald*, became Sunday editor of the *Press*. He invited me to work with him, and for several years, though I remained in the field of education, I wrote features and edited copy at the Sunday desk on Saturdays and throughout summers. This led to an opportunity to write more history. The *Press* soon developed *Wonderland*, a Sunday magazine section, and it used several of my serialized articles concerning local, state and regional history. Among them were stories about west Michigan Indians, railroads and rivers. Another, "Forts of the Unfortified Frontier," told about fortifications along both sides of the border with Canada.

Everything seemed to be going great. I was involved in educational public relations, and I was doing the kind of writing I really liked. Early in 1965, though, Wyoming voters rejected a millage increase for school operations, and my PR position was among the first things to go. Then, when the clouds seemed darkest, the sun came out. I was offered a position as director of news services and publications at Alma College. This was the answer to my career goal dream, and I spent the next twenty-four years at Alma.

After my retirement in 1989, Marty and I moved back to Grand Rapids; a few years later, we moved to Holland, where we now live.

STEPHEN P. WARD. An opportunity to do a bit more writing for an educational institution came in 2000 when Steve, then director of news and information services at Grand Valley State University, asked me to contribute articles for GVSU's alumni magazine.

LARRY J. WAGENAAR. His request (when he was director of the Holland Area Historical Society) that I serve as a member of the society's board of trustees provided another opportunity to be involved with others interested in local history. An especially competent administrator, Larry now serves as executive director of the Historical Society of Michigan. Since taking that position, he's given me the privilege of writing several stories for the society's quarterly *Chronicle* and its bimonthly *Michigan History*, a periodical previously published by the State of Michigan.

ROGER L. ROSENTRETER. During the many years *Michigan History* was published by the state, Roger was a member of its editorial staff. After writing an article for this impressive publication at the time of Alma College's centennial in 1986, I didn't submit another until January 2004, when Roger was its editor. No one could have done the job better. He was excellent with words and generous with praise. I continued writing for him and his very efficient associate, CHRISTINE SCHWERIN, until 2009, when they left the staff and control of the magazine was taken over by the historical society.

CAROLE VILADE, ANTON WISHIK and MARTY PRIMEAU. When I inquired about the possibility of writing local history articles for *Grand Rapids Magazine* in 2007, I was quickly invited aboard by Carole, editor of the publication, and Anton, who was then managing editor. Following Anton's departure from the staff, I've been privileged to work with Marty, a most capable replacement. These three have been especially pleasant to work with during the past five-plus years. Since most of the stories on the following pages first appeared in *Grand Rapids Magazine*, I can't thank them enough for their help in spreading the news of the grand times in Grand Rapids.

# Pieces of Furniture City History

## Reminders of Our First Residents

Most motorists whizzing westward on the Gerald Ford Freeway a few miles southwest of Grand Rapids aren't aware of the cluster of tree-covered mounds alongside the busy thoroughfare. Even those who venture nearer, on Indian Mounds Drive, which parallels the freeway and Grand River, don't get a really good look. Nevertheless, they form a National Historic Landmark and are considered to be the most important and best-preserved Hopewell mounds in the western Great Lakes region. And they hold clues to the culture of the area's first inhabitants.

The Hopewell people lived and farmed along major waterways in eastern North America two thousand years ago. The name they used for themselves is a mystery, but they became known as the Hopewell because their first artifacts were found on the Ohio farm of M.C. Hopewell. The earthworks at the edge of Ford Freeway were on a farm owned by Anson N. Norton at the time of their discovery, so they are known as the Norton Mounds.

Thirteen of the mounds remain at the site, which is within the boundaries of Metropolitan Park. The largest of them is eighty feet in diameter and fifteen feet high. Another group, the Converse Mounds on the west bank of the river in what is now downtown Grand Rapids, was wiped out during the 1800s by amateur archaeologists and street builders who needed fill dirt.

The Norton Mounds were excavated by archaeologists in 1874–75 and 1915, but the most extensive probing of them was done by a crew from

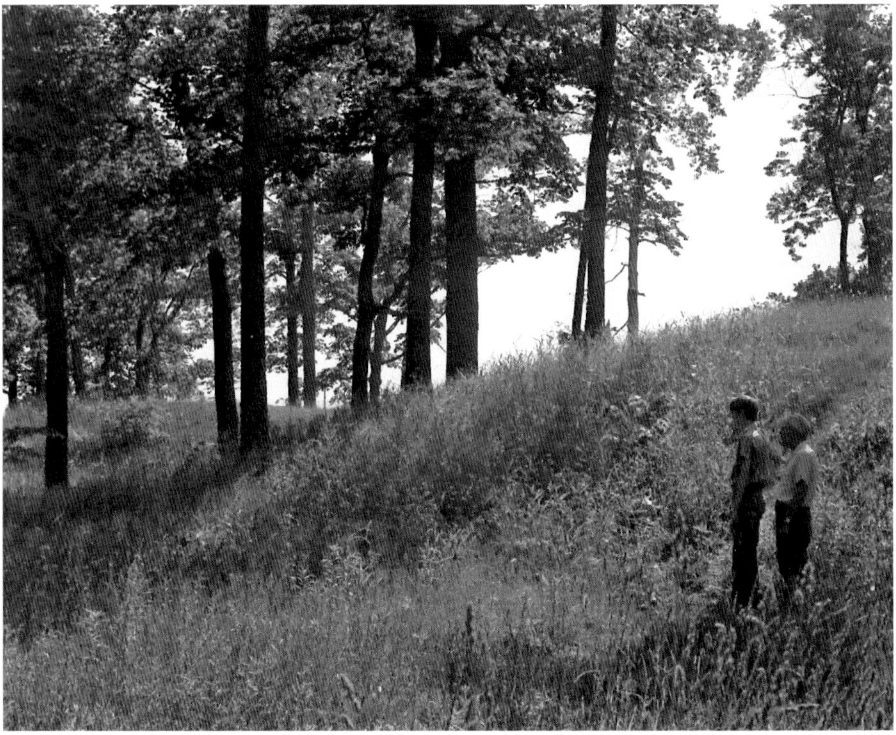

The Norton Mounds, now within Metropolitan Park, were erected by Hopewell Indians about two thousand years ago. Access to the site was permitted for many years but is now restricted until development of a master plan for long-term use is completed. *Author's collection.*

the University of Michigan's Museum of Anthropology, which opened six mounds in 1963 and then concentrated on the largest one in 1964.

Each mound had at least one skeleton of a person buried at full length. These were believed to be leaders whose deaths led to construction of the mounds. Other skeletons, which were disjointed or in hunched-up positions, were believed to be related individuals who died earlier and were removed from temporary graves to be buried with their more famous kin.

As the 1963–64 exploration of the mounds came to a close, the Grand Rapids Public Museum, which owns the site, organized the Greater Grand Rapids Indian Mounds Park Committee to consider future uses, including possible development of an interpretive center telling about the Hopewell people. A more recent step in that direction is the museum's Norton Mounds Cultural Resource Project, which has an advisory council for creating a master plan for long-term use. Until the plan is completed, access to the mounds for further study and public visits is restricted.

Inside the mounds, archaeologists found items indicating that the Hopewell carried on extensive trade: copper from Lake Superior, mica from the Carolinas and cups made from Atlantic Ocean conch shells. Among interesting items found in the 1963–64 exploration were nine dishes made from turtle shells. They had disintegrated, but when they were carefully reassembled, they were found to be engraved. One had an image of a bear, another an elk and the others geometric designs.

Corn found at Hopewell sites indicates that they relied on agriculture for part of their food supply. Bones revealed that they also hunted and fished.

By about AD 500, the Hopewell had vanished. What happened to them is a matter of considerable conjecture. Some believe that they were victims of famine, disease or an invading enemy. Some contend that the Hopewell culture attained its greatness and then merely declined as a result of apathy. What really happened? If the question can ever be answered, it will only be through further archaeological efforts and study.

## The Lady and the Sword

The sword brandished by Ethan Allen when he and his Green Mountain Boys captured Fort Ticonderoga in the early days of the American Revolution spent many years in western Michigan before making its way back to the stronghold at the eastern edge of New York State.

It was early in the morning of May 10, 1775, that Allen and his men overpowered a small garrison of British soldiers at the fort and demanded its surrender. The gate was open and the sentry asleep when they arrived. Asked by one of the British officers by what authority he demanded possession of Ticonderoga, Allen is said to have thrust the sword skyward and shouted, "In the name of the Great Jehovah and the Continental Congress!"

The fort was the first property of the British Crown to fall to the Americans during the Revolutionary War, and the cannons captured there allowed George Washington to drive the British from Boston.

After Allen's death, the sword was in possession of his son, U.S. Army captain Hannibal Montresor Allen; after he died, it was brought to Michigan by Hannibal's wife, Agnes Bodine (Lowe) Allen. Hannibal and Agnes were married in September 1808, and he died five years later at Fort Norfolk, Virginia. She became one of Eastmanville's first settlers in the mid-1830s when she came to Michigan with the family of her sister, Catherine, and her sister's husband, Benjamin Hopkins. The Hopkinses

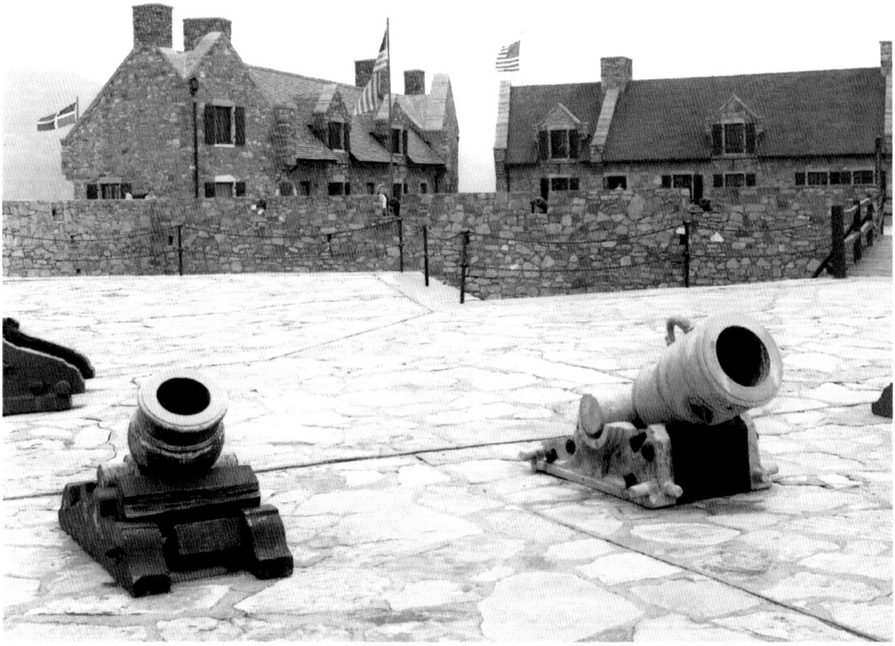

Fort Ticonderoga in New York State was captured by a sword-brandishing Ethan Allen during the Revolutionary War. His sword was eventually brought to west Michigan by his daughter-in-law, but it is presently on display at the fortification that Allen conquered. *Author's collection.*

had gone from New York to Canada in 1831 but left for Michigan during the tumultuous rebellion of 1837.

Agnes is now buried in the Hopkins plot at the Eastmanville Cemetery, beside the bodies of Benjamin and Catherine and two of their sons.

The sword, temporarily at least, is back at Fort Ticonderoga. At the Hopkins home near Eastmanville, it had hung above Agnes's desk, inside of which were the commissions issued to her husband—one as first lieutenant dated March 14, 1806, and signed by President Thomas Jefferson and the other, as captain and dated May 26, 1812, signed by President James Madison.

Described as petite, intelligent and vivacious, Agnes freely shared her views of current events and politics and has been referred to as foreshadowing the "New Woman." When Vermont officials once requested her to donate her father-in-law's sword to the state, she noted that the state had not previously cared about her husband or herself and that she had preserved the sword and would continue to do so until her death. Then it would go to whomever she chose.

At one time, the sword was displayed at the Spring Lake Masonic Lodge, where the scabbard was destroyed in a fire. The lodge had a replica made, and like the original, it has a silver band on which is inscribed "Ethan Allen, 1775." Through the years, the sword was passed on to various descendants of Hopkins relatives with whom Agnes had lived. Eventually, it was sold to a collector, who made it available for display at Fort Ticonderoga.

Agnes lived with Benjamin and Catherine Hopkins and their children both at Eastmanville and Mill Creek (now Spring Lake), where Benjamin and his sons operated a mill and general store. All except one of the family's five sons and three daughters were born in New York State before moving to Canada and Michigan.

The youngest, Mordecai, was born shortly after the others arrived in Michigan. After serving as a store clerk in Grand Haven, he joined his brothers in lumbering operations. He also was a county judge and a member of both the Michigan House of Representatives and Senate. While serving in the Civil War with the Second Michigan Cavalry, he became seriously ill and was discharged in 1862. Though an invalid, he worked for the rest of the war years as political editor of the *Chicago Times*. In 1871, he returned to Michigan and practiced law.

Though Eastmanville is now in Polkton Township, when Agnes and the Hopkins family came to the area in the 1830s, it was in what soon would become Allendale Township. Originally called Malta, the township's petition for incorporation was presented to the legislature in 1849 by Senator Henry Penoyer of Grand Haven. However, in his submission, he changed the name to Allendale, after Agnes Allen, who owned one hundred acres along Grand River just west of Allendale and was the first person listed on the 1846 tax roll.

## Persistent Paddlers

Canoeing on Grand River is something that's been going on for a long, long time. Many of us enjoy paddling up and down the river today, but long before European-born settlers came to what is now Grand Rapids, the stream was a highway for Native Americans whose villages lined its shores. Their earliest known canoes were dugouts, made by chopping or burning out the center of a log. These were followed by more complex, bark-covered craft.

Among the first non-Indian canoeists to reach Grand Rapids was Giles B. Slocum, a southeast Michigan entrepreneur who paddled downstream from

Jackson in 1834. Later, he owned extensive tracts of land on the western side of the state and, with Charles Mears, laid out the village of Whitehall.

After Charles E. Belknap came to Grand Rapids with his parents in 1846, he owned several canoes at various times and used them to pick up packs of shingles that washed off rafts as they floated down the river to Grand Haven. It was a good source of income for a boy, he said, because he was paid five cents for each bundle retrieved.

Belknap entered service in the Civil War as a private in 1862 and was discharged as a captain two years later. A volunteer fireman in the city for several years, he also was a member of the board of education and board of aldermen. After serving as mayor, he represented the area in Congress.

His favorite boyhood watercraft was a gift from a Native American whom his parents had befriended. One night, it turned up missing, but he found it among several Indian canoes at a riverside camp. Recalling the incident in his book, *The Yesterdays of Grand Rapids*, Belknap noted that he jumped into the canoe and started across the river, with several Indians in pursuit.

The *Michigan*, a steamboat, was just leaving its dock for a trip to Grand Haven; the pilot cut the engines, and crewmen used poles to push away the pursuers. Indian boys on a nearby island retaliated by shooting arrows at the steamer, and passengers on the upper deck scrambled for safety. Then, unable to reach the pursuers with their poles, the crewmen jumped ashore and threw stones.

"My canoe was lifted on deck," Belknap wrote, "and the *Michigan* swung around in the channel and steamed away for the Haven. I was afraid to be set ashore at any down river point so remained on the boat, washing dishes to pay my freight."

More peaceful canoe cruises on the Grand were commonplace at the start of the next century, when the Grand Rapids Boat and Canoe Club moved from Reeds Lake to new quarters on the bank of the river at North Park. The building, with a large ballroom and a veranda overlooking the river where regattas and other aquatic activities took place, was completed in 1908.

Sculling was also popular at the club, and some of its members were among the best in the country. At the 1912 races of the National Association of Amateur Oarsmen in Peoria, for example, Grand Rapids rowers won the intermediate four-oared shell contest, finishing ahead of teams from St. Louis and Quincy, Illinois. A year later, at the annual People's Regatta in Philadelphia, Joseph Kortlander from the Grand Rapids club was second to former Pennsylvania and Princeton star Walton Clarke in the intermediate single scull race and then teamed with Edward Shopps to take runner-up ribbons in the intermediate double scull and senior double scull events.

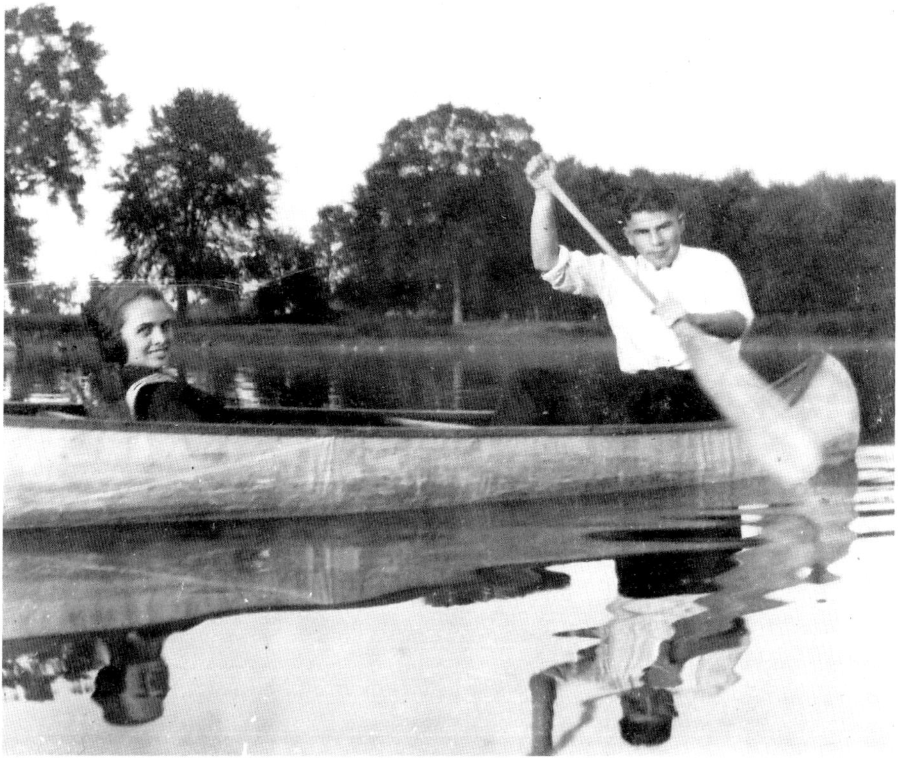

Native Americans were the first to paddle canoes in the Grand River at Grand Rapids, but when settlers from Europe arrived they also took to the water in the sleek little boats. This couple enjoyed cruising the river during the early years of the twentieth century.

The popularity of the club at North Park during the third decade of the 1900s decreased when automobiles carried greater numbers of area residents to more distant warm-weather attractions. In 1929, the City of Grand Rapids acquired the property. Today, it is the site of social activities of American Legion posts.

## Our First Businesswoman

Of the many women whose courage and determination propelled them to success in business affairs at the rapids of the Grand River, Magdelaine LaFramboise was the first. Born in 1780, she was the daughter of Marie Neskech—a child of Ottawa chief Returning Cloud and French fur trader Jean-Baptiste Marcos. Magdelaine was only three years old when her father was killed, and her mother returned with her to her native village near Grand Haven.

At the age of fourteen, Magdelaine married Joseph LaFramboise, a native of Quebec, and became a partner in his trading operations. Pioneer Grand Rapids historian Albert Baxter wrote of a report by local Indians that Joseph "established a trading post by their village at these rapids and built a cabin there, on the west side of the river, as early as about 1806."

The spring of that year is believed to have been the last time Joseph was at the rapids. He and Magdelaine spent summers at Mackinac Island, exchanging pelts for goods to be traded with Indians the following season. As the summer of 1806 neared its end, Magdelaine took her daughter, Josette, to school in Montreal. Then she and Joseph—with their infant son, also named Joseph—started out along the Lake Michigan shore toward the mouth of the Grand River.

At their last campsite, a Potawatomi village south of Muskegon, her husband was killed by an Indian in a dispute. Magdelaine ventured on, carrying the body to the Grand Haven area, where she buried it, and then

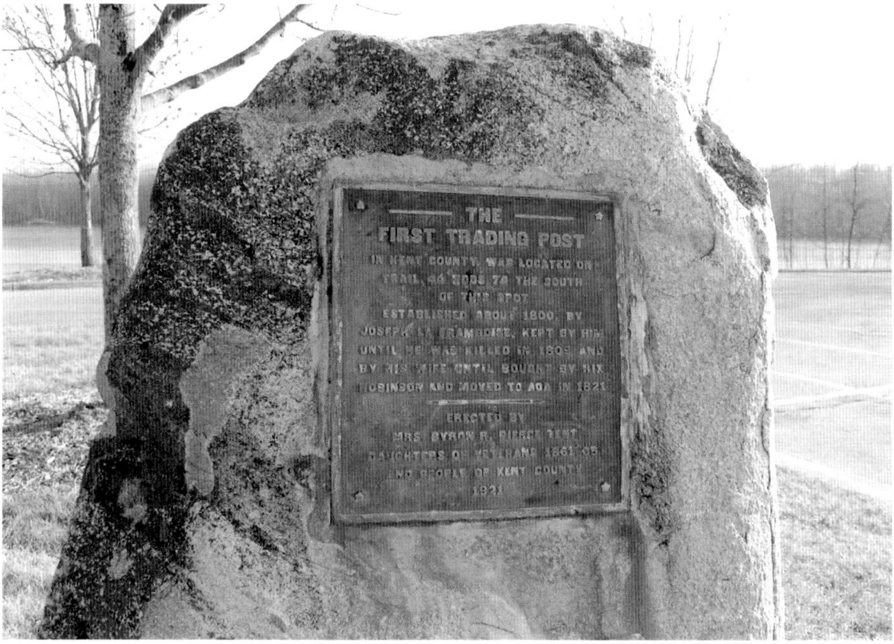


This marker at Lowell's Stoney Lake Park in eastern Kent County notes that the site of fur trading operations of Magdelaine LaFramboise was nearby. After the death of her husband, she continued his trading along the shore of Grand River for many years. *Author's collection.*

continued to their trading post just west of present-day Lowell. Several months later, Indians brought to her the man who murdered Joseph and asked how she wanted to have him killed. She said he should be forgiven and freed. Later, however, his body was found in the woods, his knife in his chest.

Magdelaine continued the business alone, usually earning between $5,000 and $10,000 per year when most traders netted only $1,000. After the War of 1812, she affiliated herself with John Jacob Astor's American Fur Company.

In April 1816, while Magdelaine was away on business, Josette married Benjamin Pierce, an army captain who had come to Fort Mackinac when the United States regained control after the war. Pierce's younger brother, Franklin, later became president of the United States. When Josette's mother returned, a grandiose ceremony and party were held on Mackinac Island.

Just four years after that marriage, Josette died, leaving a daughter, Harriet, and a young son who soon followed his mother in death. These bereavements ended Magdelaine's trading activities. She sold her business in 1822 and retired to a life of volunteer service for her Mackinac Island church, Ste. Anne's Catholic, helping to further educational opportunities for children. In the process, she herself—then in her late forties—learned to read and write in both English and French.

At her island home, Magdelaine entertained traveling dignitaries—including Alexis de Tocqueville, the French aristocrat who wrote *Democracy in America*, and Sarah Margaret Fuller, author of *Woman in the Nineteenth Century*.

In the 1820s, when Ste. Anne's needed a site for a new building, Magdelaine provided property next to her home. She and Josette are buried in the churchyard.

Magdelaine's home is now the Harbour View Inn, a small hotel complex. In September 2006, two plaques in recognition of Magdelaine's remarkable accomplishments were presented by Grand Rapids women of the Steven Preston Chapter of the United States Daughters of 1812. One is at Harbor View Inn, the other in the churchyard.

## GR's Road Feud

The street maze at the heart of downtown Grand Rapids, a puzzle to city visitors and newcomers for generations, can be traced right to the door of Louis Campau—although Lucius Lyon may deserve a bit of the blame as well. In any case, when the dust settled Grand Rapids' city center featured dead-end streets, intersections at weird angles and city "blocks" that were triangles and peculiar polygons.

Campau, an Indian trader and the city's first resident of European ancestry, had little formal education but was clever enough that the Indians called him "Wagoosh" ("The Fox"). Born in Detroit, he was one of the American soldiers turned over to the enemy by General William Hull when the British captured that city during the War of 1812. After the war, he traded with Indians on the Saginaw River and in 1826 came to the Grand River Valley.

Lucius Lyon was educated in engineering and surveying at Shelburne, Vermont, his birthplace. He came to Michigan in 1821 and was named deputy surveyor general of the Michigan Territory. Lyon later served as a delegate to Congress for the Michigan Territory, as a member of the convention that drafted the first Michigan Constitution, as a U.S. senator and as a member of the University of Michigan Board of Regents.

Both of the men wanted to buy from the government the seventy-two-acre tract now bounded by Michigan and Fulton Streets and by Division Avenue and the Grand River. Campau managed to beat Lyon to the land office at White Pigeon, and on September 20, 1831, he bought the parcel for ninety dollars.

Campau sold the northern part of his tract to Lyon, who then purchased with two associates land farther north—the tract now bordered by Michigan and Coldbrook Streets, the river and Bostwick Avenue. Both men platted their land, with Campau calling his the village of Grand Rapids and Lyon naming his the village of Kent.

The resulting feud, combined with Campau's odd street planning, created the downtown that exists today. Lyon intended that the north–south streets of his plat would connect with those of Campau's, but Campau blocked access to his area except via Division Avenue. At the northern edge of his tract, he platted a continuous row of lots along Pearl Street and placed two lots directly in the path of Canal Street (now lower Monroe Avenue), the main north–south route of Lyon's plat.

Campau sold those two lots to Abram S. Wadsworth, who promised to build a sawmill on them. But Wadsworth constructed the mill partly over the river and sold a strip to Lyon, who then extended Canal through to Pearl.

Lyon then added fuel to the fire by platting along the street that he apparently named after himself a row of lots backing up to those of Campau. The result was a "double-spite" fence extending from Division almost to the river, between Pearl and Lyon Streets.

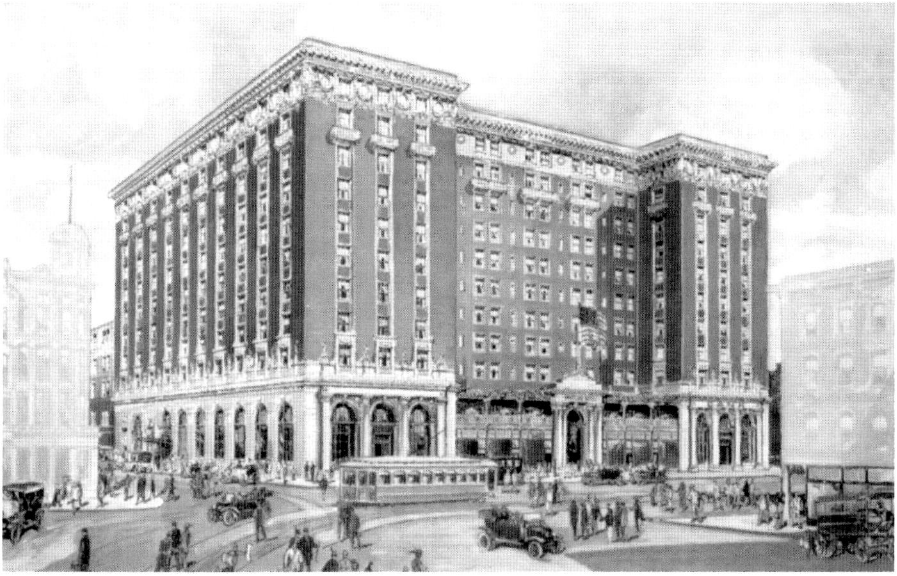

The intersection of Pearl Street at Monroe Avenue, pictured here, was at the heart of a feud between Grand Rapids pioneers Louis Campau and Lucius Lyon. Their disagreement led to a weird conglomeration of streets that has puzzled many visitors to the city for years.

Decades later, Ottawa and Ionia Avenues—the other principal north–south thoroughfares in Lyon's plat—were finally cut through to connect with the rest of downtown.

However, another aspect of Campau's street planning continues to perplex. When he laid out the village of Grand Rapids, he insisted that the main street—the part of Monroe Avenue now known as Monroe Center—follow as closely as possible an Indian trail that ran from southeast to northwest. He laid out streets on the southwest side of this thoroughfare to intersect at right angles (running southwest to northeast), but those on the northeast side of Monroe Center were built to run a true north–south. The result is the catawampus quilt of odd shapes that GR has come to know and love.

## When the Curtain Went Up

Grand Rapids hadn't yet become a city, nor Michigan a state, when the first theatrical performance was presented just a stone's throw from the rapids of the Grand River. In the late 1830s, students of the Baptist mission school on the west bank of the river performed on a hastily erected outdoor platform. When the show was slow to start and the audience became restless, actor John Peirce stuck his head through the curtain and explained, "We'll soon begin; we're fixing up a woman." The "woman" was Aaron Turner, a beardless sixteen-year-old boy.

Another notable early performance was that of an unnamed magician at the city's first entertainment hall, a building on the east bank of the river known as the Old Yellow Warehouse. When the magician deftly lifted the hat of local businessman and politician Warren Mills, nearly a peck of potatoes poured out. The crowd cheered and stamped the floor, which began to shake. With the sound of cracking timbers, the audience stormed the exit. Fortunately, the building slid only a few inches before settling, and no one was injured.

During the last half of the nineteenth century, several theaters were constructed downtown; the best known was the Powers Grand Opera House on Pearl Street, just east of Monroe Avenue. The original structure burned down but was rebuilt and endured well into the twentieth century as the Midtown Theater. During World War II, the theater was known as the Fotonews. In those days before television came to the city the Fotonews newsreels enabled audiences to see as well as hear about combat in Europe and the Pacific.

Among entertainment facilities that opened in the early decades of the 1900s were the Regent Theater, the Kent Theater, the Empress Theater (which became Keith's) and the Majestic Theater, which is now the home of the Grand Rapids Civic Theatre. At the opening of the Regent in 1923, the audience saw motion pictures of themselves as they entered the theater and sat in the auditorium.

During the first century of theater in Grand Rapids, many touring troupes and performers appeared on city stages. Spencer Tracy performed here several times with the William Wright Stock Company in the mid-1920s. Among other big names who thrilled Grand Rapids audiences were Lillian Russell, Richard Mansfield, Mary Pickford, Bela Lugosi and Ethel Barrymore. The Four Cohans—George M. and his mother, father and sister—performed at Redmond's Grand Opera House in its early days.

The Grand was especially noted for onstage thrills and special effects. William E. Clark, an usher at the Grand in the late 1800s, recalled in a 1928 *Grand Rapids Herald* story:

> *We saw people rescued from burning buildings, and real fire engines and horses dash across the stage.*
>
> *We saw shops and factories with all the machinery in operation, and a girl tied to a belt that was being slowly drawn toward the wheels.*

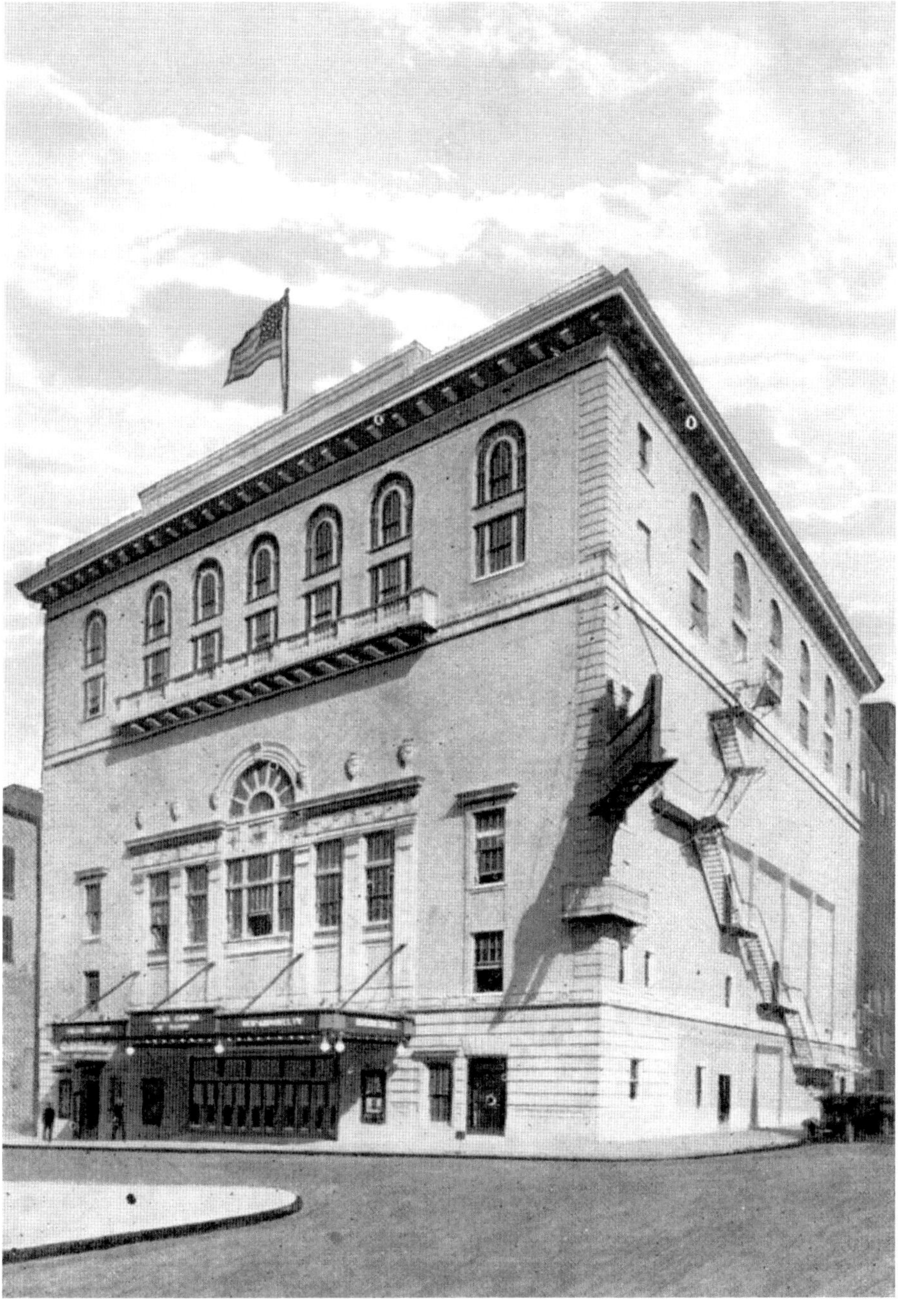

One of the many theaters where Grand Rapids couples first held hands in the dark was the Regent. At its opening in 1923, patrons saw movies of themselves, taken when they first entered the building. The downtown Regent continued to provide entertainment until 1964.

*We heard the thunder roar and saw the lightning strike, and a tornado sweep across the stage and destroy everything in its path.*

*We saw a balloon go up with real people in it.*

*We saw a threshing machine at work in a field, and a man thrown into it.*

And we think there's too much violence in the movies today!

## Like Father, Like Son

When Martin Ryerson left his home at Paterson, New Jersey, in the early 1830s and headed west, he may have had high hopes. However, his wildest dreams couldn't have matched the experiences and accomplishments that were to follow.

After a few months in Detroit, he went to Grand Rapids, where he was one of the city's earliest white settlers. Then, within a year, he moved on to Muskegon, where he became involved in trading with Indians. By the early 1840s, he had entered the lucrative lumbering business, operating sawmills and purchasing thousands of acres of pine lands along the Muskegon River and its tributaries.

At his own expense, he developed the first road out of Muskegon. With an Indian assistant, he laid out the route to Ravenna, where an existing road continued to Grand Rapids, and then hired a crew to cut out the vegetation. In the 1850s, Ryerson transferred some of his business operations to Chicago and made that his place of residence.

When he first came to Muskegon, there were few other white men in the area, and nearly all of his contacts were with Ottawa Indians. He learned their language and was greatly admired by them. After moving to Chicago, he gave the city a bronze statue of an Ottawa family, pausing as if alerted to imminent danger. It stands in Lincoln Park atop a massive granite block with four engraved panels depicting activities of the tribe, one of which has the inscription "To the Ottawa Nation of Indians, my early friends."

Though most historians record that Martin was married twice, he actually had three wives. The first, who has generally been overlooked, was an Ottawa whom he married in a tribal ceremony. She died shortly after giving birth to their only child, a daughter named Mary. Years later, at Ryerson's request, the Michigan legislature passed an act legitimizing the child.

Then he married Louisa Duverney of Grand Haven, daughter of Frenchman Pierce Duverney and his Indian wife. They had no children, and Louisa also lived but a short time. Martin then married Mary Campau;

her uncle, Louis Campau, was the first permanent settler at Grand Rapids. Their only child was Martin Antoine Ryerson, the middle name honoring his grandfather, Antoine Campau.

Martin A. attended private schools in Paris and Geneva for seven years, and he graduated from Harvard Law School in 1878. He practiced law for a few years and then joined his father in the lumbering operations in Michigan and Chicago. After his father died in 1887, Martin A. was the principal heir of his fortune. By the early 1890s, he had retired and concentrated on his philanthropic and art collecting interests. He and his closest friend, Charles L. Hutchinson, as well as their wives, traveled throughout the world in search of artistic masterpieces. Ryerson's wife, Caroline, was the daughter of the Hutchinsons.

In the early 1890s, Ryerson was involved in the formation of three great Chicago institutions: the Art Institute of Chicago, the Field Museum of Natural History and the University of Chicago. Hutchinson joined him in those efforts, and both were members of the University of Chicago's founding board of trustees in 1890. From 1892 to the early 1920s, Ryerson was president and Hutchinson treasurer of the board.

During that same period, both men devoted much of their time and treasure to the Art Institute of Chicago and served on its board. Hutchinson was at one time its president, and Ryerson was for many years the vice-president. Ryerson, said to be the greatest benefactor of the institute, gave $2 million, not including a $6 million bequest that was evenly divided among the institute, the university and the Field Museum.

Both men also were involved in the establishment of the Field Museum. Hutchinson helped to secure the site for the original building; Ryerson, who served as one of the museum's trustees for decades, obtained exhibits left after the 1892 World's Columbian Exposition for display at the facility.

Though involved in these ventures that enriched Chicago's culture, Ryerson didn't forget his hometown. In 1899, he gave Grand Rapids 3.58 acres of the old Antoine Campau farm for use as a park. It included the site of the home in which he had been born. In accepting the gift, the city council resolved that the park would be known forever as the Antoine Campau Park. Attractive plantings, well-groomed lawns and a pool with fountains made it a pleasant resting place for many years. After the city commission adopted the school-park concept in 1951, the tract became the site of Campau Park School.

Martin A. Ryerson's greatest gift to the place of his birth, however, is the downtown library that bears his name. Upon learning at the dawn of the twentieth century that voters had narrowly defeated a proposal to build a new

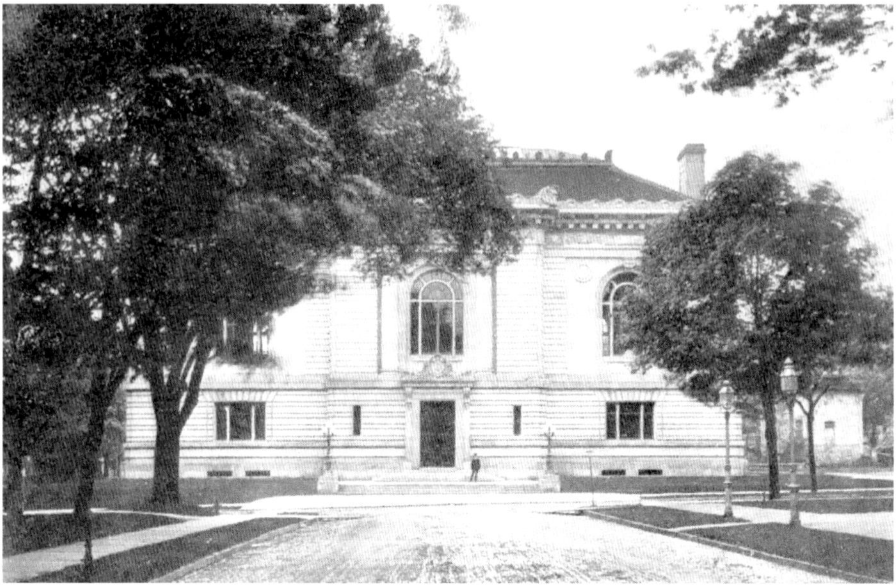

For more than a century, the Ryerson building in downtown Grand Rapids has been the city's main library facility. It was given to the city by Martin A. Ryerson, a descendant of Grand Rapids pioneers. He also was a generous benefactor of the city of Chicago.

library, he wrote to Grand Rapids officials and offered to fund construction of one if the city would provide a site. When his offer was accepted, he even supervised construction of the building, which was opened in 1904.

The Ryersons were in Grand Rapids for only a short time, but their generosity has contributed to the welfare of western Michigan residents for more than a century.

## The Pride of Wyoming

Karen Jean Southway's crowning as Miss Michigan of 1961 sent spirits soaring in her hometown, the new city of Wyoming, a half century ago.

Civic pride had mingled with anxiety during the previous few years as the former township struggled to block efforts by Grand Rapids to annex areas with high tax bases. The picture started to brighten when Wyoming became a city at the outset of January 1959 and then the site of the region's first enclosed shopping mall, Rogers Plaza, in 1960. Those accomplishments, however, didn't match the excitement generated when one of the city's own made it to the top at the Miss Michigan Pageant.

"Never at any time in the history of Wyoming," wrote Charles Vaughn and Dorothy Simon in their book, *The City of Wyoming—A History*, "has any person or event captivated the people as did the news that Miss Karen Jean Southway had won the title of Miss Michigan at the Muskegon pageant. People went wild with enthusiasm in welcoming home this charming, beautiful young lady who had suddenly become the symbol of a proud city struggling for its existence. Her victory added to the stature of Wyoming and spurred its citizens on to solve the big problems ahead."

Karen moved to Chicago after marrying Roger DeWert, whom she met when both were employed at WOOD TV in Grand Rapids. In a business that she now operates from her home in Mount Prospect, Karen is a makeup artist, pageant coach, photographer and photo editor. She's been doing that since August 1962 and has assisted hundreds of pageant contestants in their quests for crowns. Among them are five who made it to the top as Miss America.

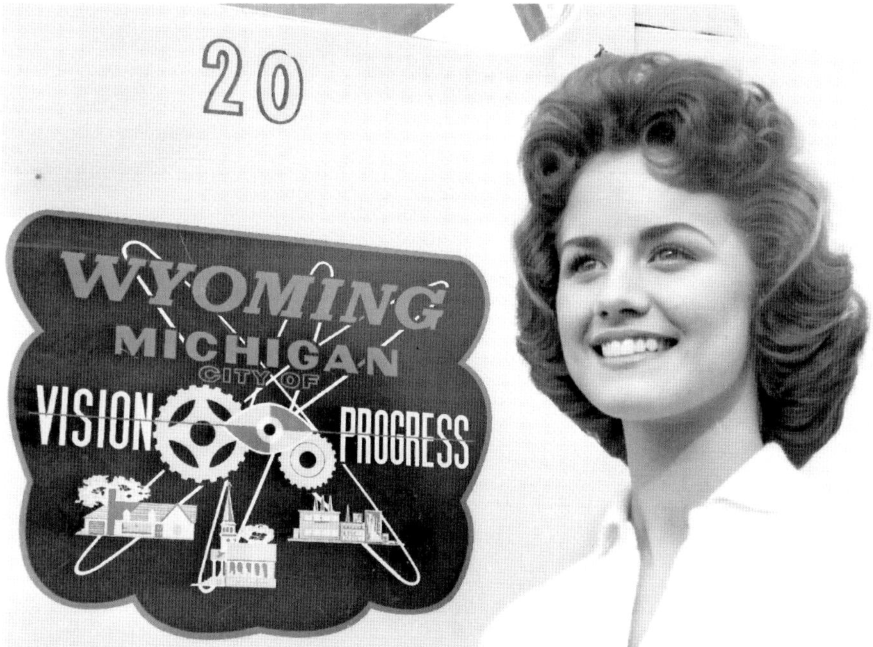


Karen Jean Southway thrilled residents of her hometown, the suburban city of Wyoming, when she was selected as Miss Michigan in 1961. Since then, she has coached hundreds of other pageant contestants, including five who became Miss America. *Author's collection.*

A year before she became Miss Michigan, Karen graduated from Rogers High School, which was named, like the plaza, for one of Wyoming's earliest settlers, Justus C. Rogers. He and his wife, Eliza, came to what is now Wyoming in the 1830s, and he began construction of a house while she stayed with friends in Grand Rapids. When it was completed, he went to the city to get her. But while he was away, Kent County's first recorded tornado swept through the area. When Mrs. Rogers first saw what was to have been her new home, it was a complete wreck.

Justus then built another, and this one still stands near the corner of Twenty-eighth Street and Michael Avenue, where it was moved to make room for Rogers Plaza. After a second story was added in 1839, the first public gathering at the home was for the double funeral of Eliza and Justus's daughters, who had died one day apart.

Wyoming was originally a part of Byron Township, which was divided in 1848, the southern portion keeping the name Byron while the northern part was named Wyoming, after a New York county that had been the home of several of the township's recent arrivals.

Unlike most municipalities, which spread out from an original center, Wyoming grew inward from the outside. It remained a mostly rural entity until the dawn of the twentieth century, when interurban transportation made suburban living more attractive and stimulated development of subdivisions and adjacent commercial districts. In 1902, the Grand Rapids, Holland and Chicago Line generated the northern Wyoming communities of Galewood, Urbandale, Burlingame, Beverly and Wyoming Park. When the Grand Rapids–Kalamazoo Line opened in 1915, the Godwin Heights and Home Acres areas were developed at the township's eastern edge. Platting of areas at the center of Wyoming didn't occur until after World War II.

The late 1940s, too, was the period when the stretch of Twenty-eighth Street—then better known as the South Beltline—between Clyde Park and Burlingame Avenues began to be considered as Wyoming's "downtown." Government offices were then moved from a rented building on Godfrey Avenue to a new township hall on the corner of Twenty-eighth and DeHoop Avenue, site of today's Wyoming City Hall and directly across Twenty-eighth from Rogers Plaza.

Just as the old South Beltline lured business from Grand Rapids during the early postwar years, recent commercial developments near the new South Beltline (M-6) and Rivertown Crossings Mall in Grandville now are pulling business away from the heart of Wyoming, and city planners are exploring possible solutions for the problem.

## A Place to Hang Your Hat

Unpretentious to say the least, when compared to magnificent hotels that now tower over downtown Grand Rapids, the first building to accommodate overnight guests in the city was a simple, twenty-six- by sixteen-foot, story-and-a-half structure.

Built at the site of present-day McKay Tower by Joel Guild in 1833, it was a home for him, his wife, six daughters and a son—and also a place where travelers could spend the night.

"I have built a framed house, the first that was ever built within a hundred miles of this place," Guild said in a December 1833 letter to New York in-laws, "and I am under the necessity of keeping [a] tavern as my house was built first. I moved into it the last day of August, and from that time to this my house has been full by day and night. Some of the time we have had twenty in the family."

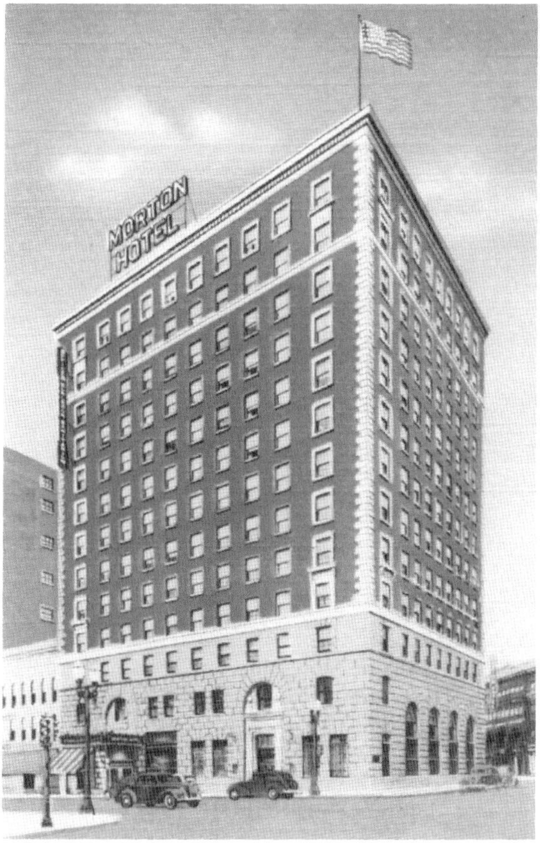


Accommodations for visitors have been provided at this downtown Grand Rapids corner since 1836, when the Hinsdale Hotel opened. Renamed the National a few years later, the building was destroyed by fire in 1872, and the Morton House was built at the site.

The first actual hotel in Grand Rapids was the Eagle, built in 1834 at the corner of Louis Street and Waterloo (now Market) Avenue. The original wooden structure burned down in 1883 and was replaced by one of brick.

The Hinsdale Hotel, which opened in 1836 at the corner of Monroe and Ionia Avenues, was renamed National Hotel a few years later. Fire destroyed the building in 1855, and the wooden structure that replaced it succumbed to flames in 1872. After that fire, a four-story brick hotel known as the Morton House was built at the site. During its days as the National, the hotel was the city's most popular, with wide verandas for relaxation in the summer and a large fireplace frequented by guests in the winter.

In his book, *The Yesterdays of Grand Rapids*, Charles Belknap recalled a boyhood experience at the National. "Ned Buntline, writer of story books for boys, was a guest at the hotel," he wrote. "The porter went out to the shops and streets and gathered in all the boys; and standing in the firelight with the youngsters sitting all about the floor, Buntline told stories of the sea and of adventure in strange lands with strange people. I was one of the happy boys."

A few years later, Belknap joined the Union army at age fifteen and became a captain at seventeen. He was a lieutenant colonel when he was mustered out. Back in civilian life, he was mayor of Grand Rapid and a U.S. congressman. Buntline, creator of the dime novel, led a life as adventurous as those of the characters in his stories. He also entered military service at age fifteen when he became a navy midshipman. At twenty-three, accused of murder and lynched by a mob in Tennessee, he cheated death when others cut him down from the hanging tree.

Belknap also recorded memories of hotel manager Canton Smith's wife, who reached out to help the unfortunate. "The fireplace in the lobby," Belknap wrote, "was matched by the warmth of the stove in the kitchen on which a kettle of soup ever simmered and from which many a bum was fed and sent away to the hay in the stables. There were no city hospitals or refuge homes—only the county house to shelter unfortunate girls from the storm—and many a friendless woman was helped up the back stairs to the servants quarters and a bed."

Owners of the new hotel when it opened as the Morton House in 1874 were Farnham L. Lyon and A. Vorhis Pantlind, whose nephew, J. Boyd Pantlind, was a bellboy, porter and clerk. The younger Pantlind became owner of the Morton in the 1890s and later purchased Sweet's Hotel, which he remodeled and renamed the Pantlind. It had 125 rooms at the time. Further remodeling projects, most impressive of which was completed in time for a New Year's Day 1916 formal opening, increased the number of rooms to 550. Later, the hotel was managed by J. Boyd's son, Fred Z. Pantlind, and was regarded in the mid-1920s as one of America's ten finest hotels. The Pantlind is now the east wing of the twenty-nine-story Amway Grand Plaza Hotel.

## Road to the White House

The first presidential election in the village of Grand Rapids didn't come close to matching the excitement of today's campaigns. There wasn't even a newspaper to proclaim the virtues of the candidates.

Michigan was still a territory in 1836 when the city first became a presidential polling place—the only voting place in Kent County. Without enough voters to warrant speeches and rallies, there was no hoopla that year; fifty-four of the sixty-one votes cast in the county went to Martin Van Buren, who defeated William Henry Harrison to become the country's eighth president.

It wasn't for another fifty-two years—October 22, 1878—that a future president actually visited the city. James A. Garfield, who would be elected president two years later, came to Grand Rapids to speak at the Powers Opera House. After the address, he went to the home of his brother, Thomas, who lived near Jamestown in Ottawa County.

Notes of an interview with Thomas, recorded by hand in 1894 and later given to the Grand Rapids Public Library, indicate that President Garfield was not as ambitious in his youth as is claimed by Encyclopedia Americana, which notes: "James's childhood was one of hardship and work. The last President to be born in a log cabin, Garfield had little leisure time in his youth. He did farm work until he was sixteen years old, then found employment on a canal boat." But Thomas told the interviewer, "He could do anything but hoe corn and that he wouldn't do, and he wouldn't chop wood either…And if I scolded him for cutting off the corn instead of the weeds, he would throw down his hoe and go to the house and take up a book." The older brother admitted that James did work on the canal but said that it was only for one trip when he was a teenager.

Four months after his inauguration in 1881, President Garfield was assassinated by a disgruntled office-seeker.

William McKinley spoke twice in Grand Rapids before becoming president: in 1890 as a congressman and in 1894, when he was governor of Ohio. His opponent for the presidency in 1896, William Jennings Bryan,

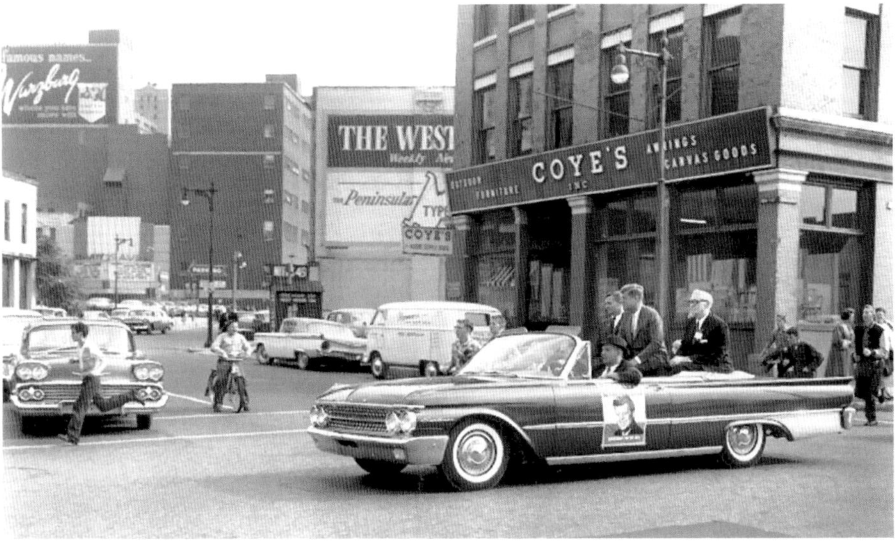


President John F. Kennedy rides through downtown Grand Rapids during the 1960 campaign. The first future president to seek votes in the city was James A. Garfield, who came in 1878 and, after his appearance here, visited his brother, Thomas, in nearby Ottawa County. *Courtesy of Grand Rapids History and Special Collections, Archives, Grand Rapids Public Library.*

made three speeches in the city on October 15 of that year, attracting crowds to Campau Square, Powers Opera House on Pearl Street and the Auditorium at the corner of Ionia Avenue and Fountain Street.

In September 1900, Theodore Roosevelt, then a candidate for the vice presidency, came to Grand Rapids and was escorted to the Auditorium by a troop of his Spanish-American War Rough Riders. Bryan, again the Democratic candidate for president, returned to Grand Rapids in October to speak at Campau Square and the Auditorium. A week later, his running mate, Adlai E. Stevenson, spoke at Campau Square.

Another vice presidential candidate, Republican senator Charles W. Fairbanks of Indiana, spoke in Grand Rapids during the 1904 campaign. He and Roosevelt, who had assumed the presidency after the assassination of McKinley, were elected. Roosevelt returned to the city in 1911 to speak at a Lincoln Day dinner.

A sitting chief executive didn't come to Grand Rapids until William Howard Taft arrived in September 1911, a year before the end of his administration. Besides speaking at Campau Square, he made several other appearances, including one at the Ladies Literary Club. There he referred to the ladies, who did not yet have the right to vote, as "the real governing body" and added, "Whether you govern through your fathers, husbands or brothers, I cannot determine, but through them your power is felt."

Woodrow Wilson was in Grand Rapids in 1912 shortly before becoming the Democratic nominee, and in 1916 his opponent for the presidency, Charles Evans Hughes, spoke in the city. Herbert Hoover made the first of two Grand Rapids appearances in 1920.

One president's involvement with the city was a long-distance affair. Calvin Coolidge turned on the lights to open the 100th semiannual Grand Rapids Furniture Market in January 1928. The switch was located in the White House, and the *Grand Rapids Press* reported that "his impulse with the speed of light hurried through telegraph wires to a master switch in the city powerhouse and down Monroe Avenue."

Contenders came in rapid succession during October 1936, when President Franklin D. Roosevelt began his speech at Campau Square one hour after Republican nominee Alfred M. Landon's train pulled out of Union Station. A crowd of 150,000 greeted FDR, clogging Monroe Avenue.

Roosevelt's 1940 opponent, Wendell Willkie, came to Grand Rapids in October of that year. Harry S Truman, who assumed the presidency after FDR's death in 1945, addressed a Campau Square crowd in September 1948.

Both John F. Kennedy and Richard M. Nixon were speakers at the square in 1960. Robert F. Kennedy thrilled a crowd there in April 1968, two months before an assassin's bullet ended his campaign for the Democratic nomination.

Most presidential candidates have campaigned in Grand Rapids in recent years, but none was as enthusiastically welcomed as the city's favorite son, Gerald R. Ford, who was here twice in 1976. During a springtime primary battle with Ronald Reagan, President Ford came to Grand Rapids after an appearance at Holland's Tulip Time. He and wife Betty came back in November to cast their ballots at Wealthy Elementary School.

## From Defeat to Delight

The failure by eastern investors to develop a metropolis and Lake Michigan port in Ottawa County during the 1830s provided Grand Rapids with a bundle of architectural treasures: four majestic Greek columns that, for more than a century and a half, have adorned an East Fulton Street building.

Earlier, they stood at the front of a hotel in Port Sheldon, a short-lived city that its creators thought would become what Chicago is today. The Port

Sheldon Company, established at Philadelphia in 1835, bought six hundred acres on the north shore of Pigeon Lake from the federal government for just $900 and began efforts to transform the site in the wilderness into a thriving commercial center.

Gravel roads, said to be the only ones west of Detroit and north of Ohio and Indiana, were built from Port Sheldon to Grand Haven and Grandville. The plat of the city had 142 blocks, each with twenty-four lots that were 62 by 128 feet. One lot was reserved for a school, three for markets, seven for churches and four each for a city hall and a railroad depot. The depot, with a gilded sign and a roof supported by Grecian columns, was soon erected, and three miles of roadbed were laid to the east. Also built were a lighthouse and piers along the Pigeon Lake shore, a general store, a company office, a steam sawmill and the Ottawa House, a two-story, twenty-nine-room hotel.

Painted white, the eighty- by one-hundred-foot Ottawa House was an impressive structure, with six Grecian columns at the front. It was opened on December 1, 1838, but its business never matched its appearance. During the years its rooms were available, 1838–43, only 112 guests registered.

On paper, Port Sheldon looked good. But its planning was poor, and within a few years the venture had failed. The city had a fancy railroad

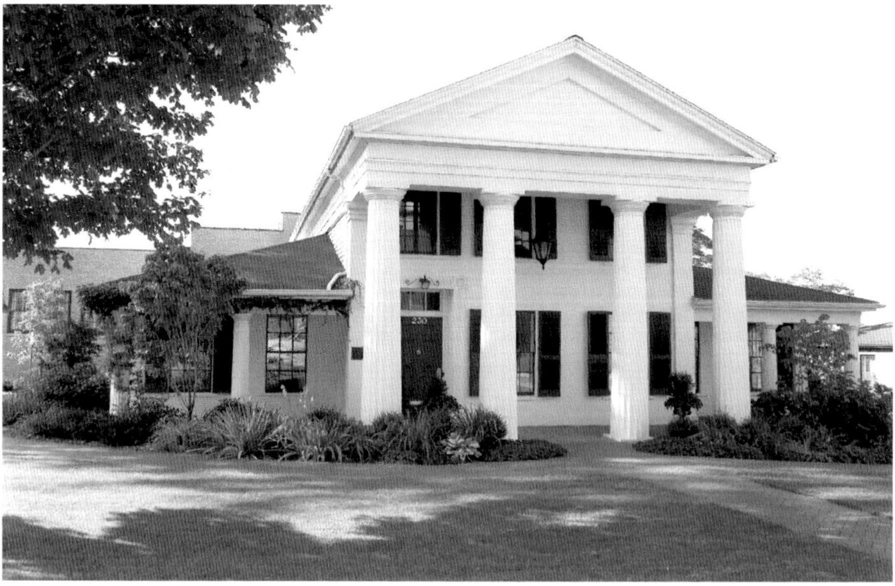

The four large columns of this building at the eastern edge of downtown once stood at the front of a hotel erected in the 1830s at the Lake Michigan shore. It was the most impressive structure in a development intended to rival Chicago, but when the venture failed, the pillars were hauled through the forest to Grand Rapids by oxen. *Author's collection.*

depot, but there were no tracks for trains to reach it. There was a lighthouse and piers, but the channel between Lake Michigan and Pigeon Lake would completely close when storms filled it with sand. And when it was open, the channel had insufficient width or depth for ships to enter the port. The sawmill was one of the best in the region, and there was plenty of timber to cut. But it did little business because neither ships nor trains could get near enough to pick up timber that would be cut. Though it was an attractive building, the Ottawa House was, as an 1891 *Detroit Free Press* history of Port Sheldon pointed out, a "hotel in the wilderness where a traveler did not come once a month."

So all work on the project stopped, and the Port Sheldon Company began to dispose of its assets. Abram Pike, company clerk, stayed at the site for a few years to care for the property and sell whatever he could. In 1844, when he moved to Grand Rapids, he had four of the six Ottawa House pillars hauled through snowy forests by teams of oxen and used them as an impressive architectural feature of the home he built on East Fountain Street.

The pillars are believed to have been made in Detroit and were transported on scows to Port Sheldon in 1836. Smaller pillars at side porticos of the Pike House came from the Port Sheldon Depot. The building at 230 East Fulton Street served as the Grand Rapids Art Gallery (now Grand Rapids Art Museum) for more than fifty years, 1924–80. Presently, it houses offices of an architectural and engineering company.

Port Sheldon became a popular resort community in 1906 when fifteen Grand Rapids men formed the Port Sheldon Beach Association and purchased property on the south shore of Pigeon Lake. Since 1960, the site of the failed metropolis on the north side of the lake has been occupied by the huge Campbell Generating Complex of Consumers Energy.

## Steamin' Along on the Grand

It's been nearly a century since the sound of steamboat whistles echoed between buildings along the Grand River shore at Grand Rapids, but for many years, the steamers churned the water downriver to Grand Haven and upstream to Lyons.

The first of them was the *Governor Mason*, a side-wheeler that made a trial run to Grandville on the Fourth of July in 1837. But it had no whistle, and a bugler was needed to signal its arrivals and departures. The ship's engine and boiler had been used on the *Don Quixote*, a boat that was wrecked in Lake

Huron while carrying a printing press for the first Grand Rapids newspaper, the *Grand River Times*. Builders of the *Governor Mason* reportedly borrowed $2,000 from two Indian chiefs to purchase the power essentials.

Though the rapids prevented most steamships from operating both upstream and down, the *Mason*, after sailing the lower part of the river, did manage to go upstream to Lyons in December 1837. High water in the river—combined with tugging by horses, oxen and twenty Indians—managed to get the boat through the rough stretch.

Though deep water was helpful on that occasion, a few months later it resulted in the *Mason* taking an unscheduled and unfortunate voyage. A freshet tore the boat loose from its dock and carried it along flooded terrain several blocks to the east of the river. When the water receded, considerable cash and effort were needed to return the *Mason* to the stream. Two years later, the boat ventured into Lake Michigan and was blown ashore and wrecked at the mouth of the Muskegon River.

A second steamer, the *Owashtanong*, also began sailing the Grand in 1837. This one did have a whistle, claimed by its designer to be the first one made in Michigan west of Detroit. "I waited until we got well out of town before I tried it," he said. "We were down near the log school house a short distance downstream, and the children heard it and were afraid to go to school because they thought it was a panther howling in the woods."

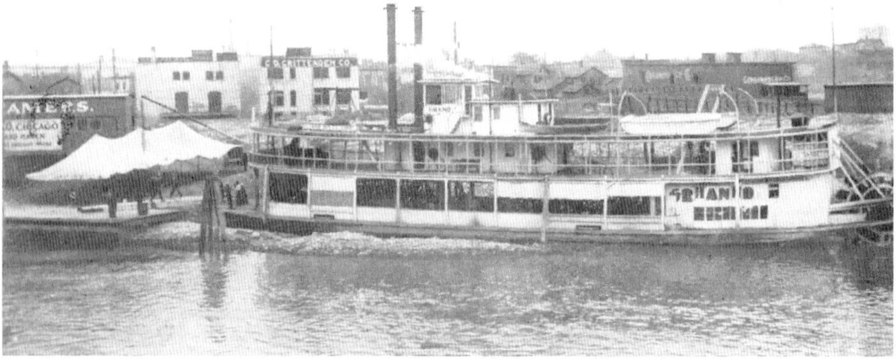

The *Grand*, one of the last of more than forty riverboats that carried passengers and freight between Grand Rapids and Grand Haven, is pictured at its downtown dock in the early 1900s. The *Grand* and its twin stern-wheeler, the *Rapids*, were built in an unsuccessful last-ditch effort to keep steamboat service on Grand River alive.

During the next eighty years, more than forty steamboats operated on the Grand, most of them on the downriver route between the rapids and Grand Haven, but a few sailed the stretch above the rapids to Lyons. Flat bottoms and shallow drafts in these watercraft made it possible for them to sail in sections of the river that would not have been navigable for boats requiring deep water. The typical shipping season, from March through November, sometimes was extended by warmer than usual weather.

One of the better-known steamships on the Grand was the *Humming Bird*, built in 1847 at Lamont. Historian Albert Baxter described it as a boat "on two canoes with a single paddle wheel in the middle." Another was the *William H. Barrett*, which sailed the river for twenty years after it was built at Grand Rapids in 1874. Sparks from its stack started an 1893 fire at Spring Lake that destroyed much of the village's east side. A year and a half later, the *Barrett* itself burned while moored in Grand Rapids.

The *May Graham* was the last steamer to make the run between Grand Rapids and Grand Haven, passing through the swing bridge at Eastmanville shortly before it rusted shut about 1917. After being disassembled, it was used as a barge. Its pilothouse and upper decks served as a cottage at Grand Haven until the 1950s.

Though it may seem that Eastmanville's rusty bridge was the villain that ended steamboat travel on the Grand, rail transportation was the real culprit. Steam-driven trains reached Grand Rapids and Grand Haven in 1858, and electric interurbans came in at the start of the twentieth century.

Investors at Grand Rapids tried to keep steamboat operations alive and built two stern-wheel replicas of Mississippi riverboats in 1905. Named the *Grand* and the *Rapids*, they started sailing between Grand Rapids and Grand Haven the following year, but competition by interurban lines forced their sale in 1912.

Today, the diesel-powered *Grand Lady* offers summertime cruises between its dock at Grandville and Grand Haven, but the steamers that once sailed the river are no more than cherished memories for a few old-timers.

## Bridging the Grand

The Grand River and its rapids may have given the city its name, but this longest of Michigan's streams split the community and hindered social and commercial activity until the mid-1800s when bridges first linked the east and west sides. Before then, only canoes and other small boats provided passage between the two shores.

The first opportunity to cross the river without the help of paddles and oars came in 1842 when a footbridge was erected just south of today's Bridge Street span. Three years later, with funds from the state, the city constructed the first bridge suitable for traffic at Bridge Street. This span, which could support wagons, lasted until the Grand Rapids Bridge Company was formed in 1852 and replaced it with a covered toll bridge.

A spectacular fire—with a roaring sheet of flames that quickly spread more than eight hundred feet across the river—destroyed that bridge and several commercial buildings at its east end in April 1858. Replacement began almost immediately, and a hastily constructed footbridge served pedestrians until the new span was completed in September. A month later, construction of a bridge at Leonard Street was completed, and in November another opened at Pearl Street.

All three of the new bridges were covered and charged tolls. Typical of fees for crossing the river were those at Bridge Street, where charges were one penny for pedestrians, two cents for horseback riders, three cents for wagons pulled by a single horse and four cents for wagons pulled by a team of horses. The Bridge Street bridge provided a favorite promenade for courting couples from the east side who would walk across and then, just a few feet from the frustrated toll taker at the west end, turn around and go back without paying for the crossing.

Just before the fall completion of the three new spans, another also was put in service. This one, between Leonard and Ann Streets, was built by the Detroit and Milwaukee Railroad, which that summer provided the city's first connection to the rest of the world by rail.

When troops returned from Civil War service in 1865, Pearl Street's bridge was the site of one of the city's grandest parties. On the Fourth of July that year, a table, filled with food prepared by Grand Rapids ladies, extended from one end of the 620-foot span to the other. More than one thousand people enjoyed the feast.

In the early 1870s—when the spans at Leonard, Bridge and Pearl Streets were purchased by the city—tolls were eliminated. Through the years, the old bridges were replaced by more modern structures, and several others were constructed. Added were bridges at North Park, Fulton, Sixth, Wealthy and Ann Streets, along with the more recent ones that carry freeway traffic over the river. Several more railroad bridges eventually crossed the Grand, too.

Fire wasn't the only threat to early Grand Rapids bridges. In March 1881, heavy ice in the river slammed into Bridge Street Bridge and destroyed a section at the east end. Two years later, thousands of logs,

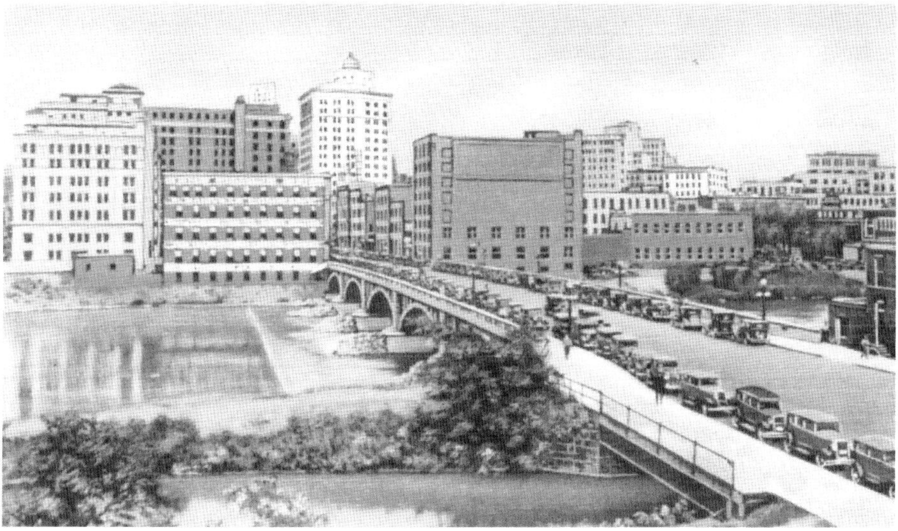

Besides connecting the east and west sides of the city, bridges in Grand Rapids have served as parking lots, promenades for courting couples and picnic grounds. This is Pearl Street Bridge at the heart of the city in the 1930s.

held upstream by a boom, broke loose and swept down the river until they became wedged against the Detroit, Grand Haven and Milwaukee Railroad Bridge. The resulting timber jam was said to be thirty feet high and seven miles long. Thousands came to the river for a view of the spectacle, and some of the more daring—or careless—even ventured out onto the logs. Eventually, the pressure wiped out three hundred feet of the bridge at its west end; the logs continued downstream, demolishing two more railroad spans. The city's other bridges were only slightly damaged.

Though most of the older Grand Rapids bridges have disappeared, a few remain, and vehicles are still able to cross some of them. Two of the most popular old spans, however, are limited to pedestrian traffic. One, now known as the Blue Bridge, is the oldest of the remaining railroad bridges in the city. Built in 1892 for the Grand Rapids and Indiana Railroad, it's used today by downtown walkers to cross the river between Pearl and Fulton Streets.

The other, located north of Pearl, was built in 1915 to enable cars of two interurban lines, linking Grand Rapids with Holland and Kalamazoo, to cross the river. Recently named the Richard Gillette Memorial Bridge, it spans the river between DeVos Performance Hall and Ah-Nab-Awen Park.

## FIGHTING THE FIRST FIRES

The city's first fire engine, perhaps impressive when it was created, wouldn't catch an admiring glance today. It was developed after fire leveled the Kent County Courthouse in July 1844 when citizens determined that something had to be done to protect property and life.

As a result, local manufacturer William Peasley designed and built a hand engine called a "tub." The device amounted to a box six feet long, two and a half feet wide and fifteen inches deep, as well as set on four wheels so that it could be dragged to blazes by firemen. With four men on each side pushing handles up and down, a pump in the bottom of the rig forced water through a short line of hose and a nozzle. Since there was no intake line, water needed to be provided from the closest source by means of a bucket brigade. A double line between the available water and the fire was formed, with one row passing the filled buckets and the other returning the empties.

Historians Dwight Goss and Albert Baxter claimed that the machine could throw a stream of water over a three-story building. But Charles E. Belknap, a Grand Rapids fireman before and after his service in the Union army during the Civil War, pointed out one of its deficiencies. Since the river

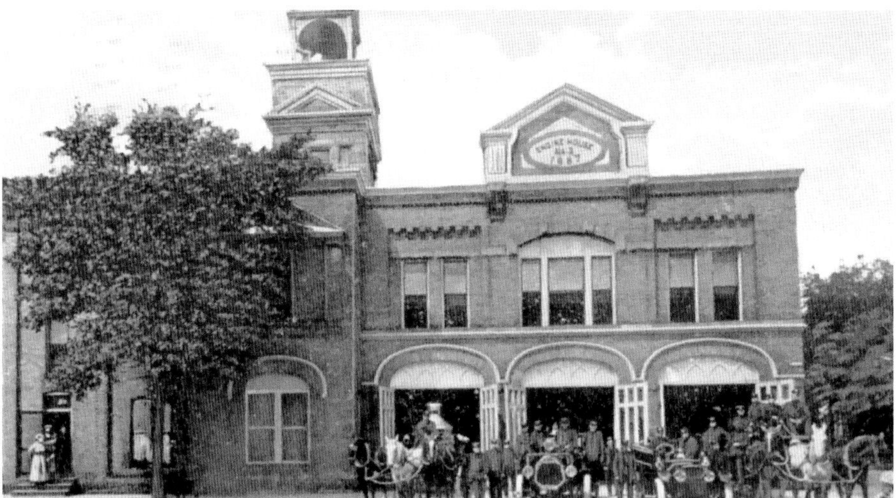

Horse-drawn and motorized units were lined up in front of Engine House No. 3 for this picture in the early 1900s. Horror and humor sometimes mingled in the early days of Grand Rapids firefighting. On one occasion, when kegs of whiskey and pails of paint were rescued from a burning building, firemen became dizzy and decorated.

often was the water source, "once, a red-fin mullet choked the pump," he said, "and before they got the fish out, the building was a total loss."

A decade later, Grand Rapids had seventy-three unpaid firemen in three fire companies, three hand-operated engines, three hose carts, 250 feet of hose and a few ladders. Company No. 1 was based in the Prospect Hill schoolhouse until it was moved to the basement of a building at Monroe and Ottawa Avenues. Company No. 2 had a rented room at the corner of Ionia and Fountain Streets, and No. 3 operated from its station at Front and First Streets on the city's West Side.

The three companies responded to one of the city's most destructive early fires on September 25, 1857, when twenty-five structures were leveled on Canal, Monroe and Ottawa Avenues in the heart of town.

According to Belknap, there was a bit of humor amid the devastation. "From one of the stores, many large boxes of dry paints were carried into the street," he said. "Every store kept whisky in those days, and none of them drinking water. As a result, the male population (firemen), thirsty and hard pressed by the flames, got a little dizzy and began tumbling into the paint boxes. Yellows and greens and purple began to blend with the blue and gray of smoke and ashes. If any of you have a desire to know how funny a man really can look, fill his inside with fire water and his outside with the colors of the rainbow."

The early historians contend that the men of No. 1 and No. 2 companies—those who were mixed up with whiskey and paint—were demoralized by evening. The crew from No. 3 battled the fire throughout the night. To express their appreciation to the men who remained sober, women of the town presented Company No. 3 with a silk banner. Painted on it was a picture of the group's chief and its hand engine, along with an expression of appreciation.

Arsonists were active in the early days. Two were arrested in 1873. A man set two blazes, one of them leveling several buildings on both sides of Monroe Avenue. After his confinement, threatening words by the police chief prompted the firebug to leave town and never return. The other arsonist was a woman who set fire to a neighbor's chicken coop during a West Side dispute. Several nearby homes also went up in flames, and the lady departed for a lengthy stay in the House of Correction at Detroit.

Five years later, imprisonment preceded arson. At four o'clock on a January morning, inmates at the county jail set fire to the building. Quick responses by the sheriff and firemen held the damage to $10,000.

## Women Started It All

Grand Rapids was still in its infancy when small groups of women, concerned about the welfare of the ill and unfortunate in their community, took the initial steps leading to an establishment of the city's earliest general hospitals.

It was December 1846 when a few ladies met in a schoolhouse at Prospect Hill and decided that they should reach out to those who needed help. At that time, Grand Rapids covered only forty acres and had a population of about 1,500. Prospect Hill, a sixty-foot-high mound that covered a large part of today's downtown, has vanished. Through the years, its soil was removed to fill in low spots and level nearby streets.

A few weeks after the schoolhouse conference, the Female Union Charitable Association was formed with a goal of helping the sick and needy; clothing children for day and Sunday schools; and encouraging habits of thrift, industriousness and cleanliness. During the years that followed, as its members cared for the city's unfortunate, the name of the association and location of its activities frequently changed. It was incorporated as the Grand Rapids Orphan Asylum Association in 1858 and, at that time, operated in a small house on Prospect Avenue.

In 1873, when it was renamed the Union Benevolent Association (UBA), a charter was adopted providing for "all kinds of benevolent work, and with

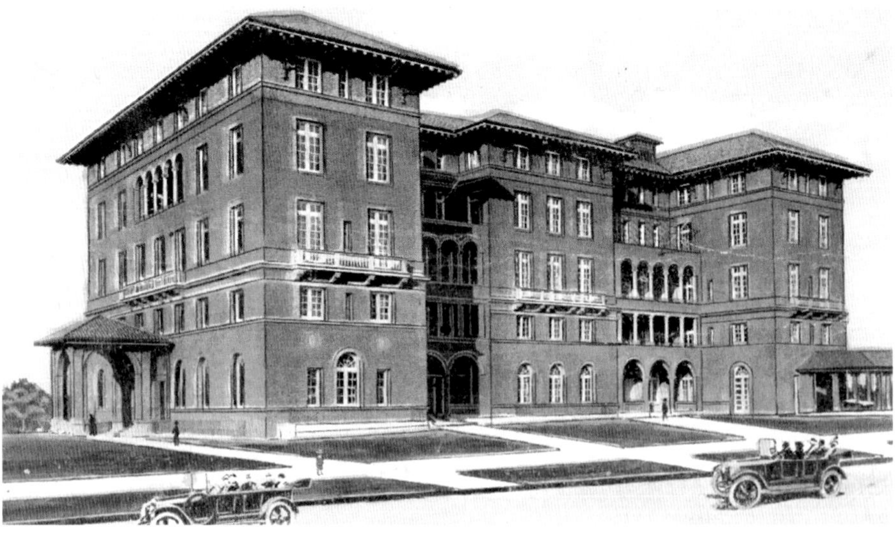

Spectrum Blodgett Hospital began providing medical care for Grand Rapids area residents in 1916. John W. Blodgett, president of the Union Benevolent Association, provided funds for its construction in honor of his mother, Jane Wood Blodgett.

the privilege of maintaining and managing a home and a hospital for the aged, the infirm, the sick, and the needy." A house on Bostwick Avenue near Lyon Street then became the base of operations for several years.

Early in the next decade, when it became obvious that a larger building was needed, the association's trustees decided to seek funds for erecting a structure on property at the corner of College Avenue and Lyon Street that had been purchased in 1869. The new UBA Hospital was opened on February 23, 1886. Three years later, a home for nurses was built, and a two-year course in nursing was provided, with instruction by the city's physicians.

When Dr. Charles Shepherd, president of the UBA for its first thirty-five years, died in 1893, he was succeeded by Thomas D. Gilbert, who several years earlier had provided funds to wipe out the entire $8,000 debt of the association. The UBA's next president, John W. Blodgett, donated funds for construction of a new hospital in the triangle of land bordered by Plymouth Road and Wealthy and Sherman Streets. Opened in 1916, it was given in honor of his mother, Jane Wood Blodgett, and was known as Blodgett Memorial Hospital.

Another local hospital grew from the efforts of Reverend Samuel Earp, rector of St. Mark's Episcopal Parish, and eight ladies of the church who, in 1873, established a home for care of a few older members of the congregation. That year, one of the members of the founding group, Mrs. Edward P. Fuller, and her husband provided a home on Bond Avenue south of Crescent Street and, in 1875, a larger one on Island (now Weston) Street. In 1876 the home was incorporated as St. Mark's Home and Hospital.

In 1887, Richard E. Butterworth gave St. Mark's a building site at the southwest corner of Michigan Street and Bostwick Avenue. He died the following year but left another gift to make possible the construction of a new hospital. It was opened in April 1890, and a school for nurses was completed by 1893. A year later the facility was renamed Butterworth Hospital.

Butterworth's grandson, Edward Lowe, and his wife made several generous gifts to the hospital in the early 1900s; in 1921, they donated the city block bounded by Michigan, Bostwick, Crescent and Ransom plus $500,000 toward a building fund. Grand Rapids citizens gave an additional $500,000, and the new hospital was opened in May 1925.

Women also were largely responsible for the establishment of Saint Mary's Hospital, which was opened by the Sisters of Mercy at a house on Lafayette Avenue given in 1893 by Mrs. Mary McNamara. To manage the facility, three nuns came that year from a hospital in Big Rapids where they had cared for men injured while lumbering. Acquisition of additional nearby property enabled expansion, and a school for nurses was added before the end of the nineteenth century. In 1911, a five-story hospital was completed at the corner of Lafayette and Cherry Street.

Prospect Hill and its schoolhouse vanished long ago, but the steps that were taken there in 1846 by a few Grand Rapids women changed and lengthened the lives of thousands in the city, and they continue to do so.

## Winters of Yesterday

Today, some of us recall old-time winters with a lot of frigid air and deep snow, and we blame—or credit—global warming for unseasonably warm days. However, the winters of bygone days didn't always have constantly cold air and a lot of snow.

Albert Baxter, who summarized winter weather at Grand Rapids from 1833 to 1889 in his *History of the City of Grand Rapids*, wrote that in 1837–38 January was so warm that men plowed in the fields and navigated the lakes. He added that "the whole of March was like summer."

On the other hand, his records show that during the winter of 1842–43 two feet of snow fell on November 18, and the ground was white until mid-April. And in 1874–75, there were "high winds and drifting, impeding railway trains, the temperature going down to 22 degrees below zero on February 7 and to 36 degrees below on February 9. Trains were snowbound for several days in the following week, and farm roads were drifted to the top of the fences in many places, while in some railroad cuts the snow banks were from ten to fifteen feet deep."

In those days of the nineteenth century, skating was the activity most appealing to winter sports enthusiasts at Grand Rapids, women and men alike. The city's first artificial rink was made in 1868 by flooding a tract just north of Bridge Street near Broadway Avenue, and a band of musicians often added to the merriment. In exceptionally cold weather, however, Grand River sometimes was completely covered with ice and provided a natural rink at the heart of town.

In his book of early reminiscences, *The Yesterdays of Grand Rapids*, Charles Belknap recalled that most of the skates when he was a teenager were homemade. When the Dutch came to the city, he said, they brought their skates and skating attire. "Our American girls wore long skirts and trim shoes," he continued, "while the Holland girls dressed in short corduroy skirts, heavy wool stockings, and stout shoes that supported the ankle."

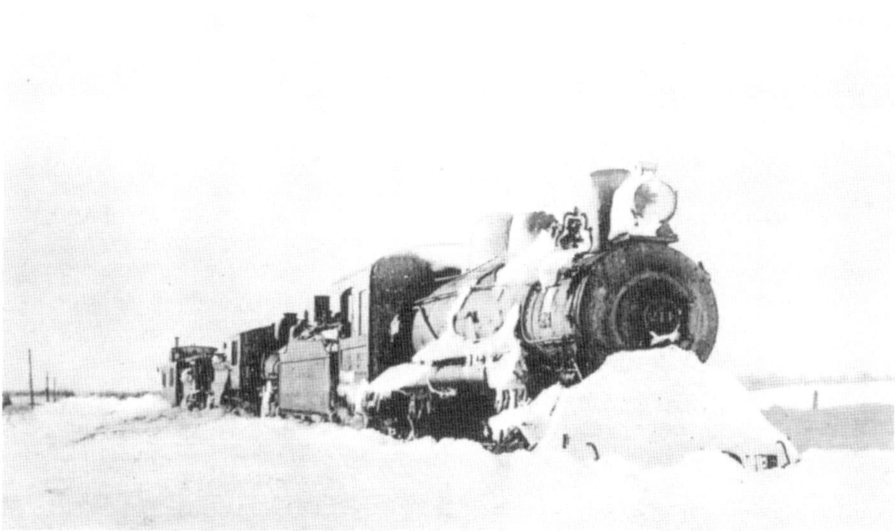

Powerful locomotives, like this one stalled in the snow between Grand Rapids and Holland, were sometimes halted by Michigan storms in railroading's early days. At the other extreme, warm winters sometimes enabled farmers to plow their fields in January.

Belknap, who was a Grand Rapids mayor and later a member of Congress, told of an occasion when skating on the Grand was exceptionally exciting, when "all the skaters in town were out." Though there were large islands of ice suitable for skating, some of the openings between them presented challenges to the more daring skaters. One of the gaps appeared to be slightly wider than could be jumped, but a group of Dutch girls sped across the ice, and "going into the air one by one in their short skirts they cleared the glade and landed safely on this island of temptation."

Several "American boys," as Belknap called them, managed to cross as well and soon "were linked arm in arm with the rosy-cheeked, sensibly dressed Netherlands girls." That displeased the lady friend of one of the young men. After spotting him cavorting with an attractive blond Hollander, she determined to leap over the open water and put an end to it. But her skate caught in her long skirt, and she plunged into the river and under the ice.

Men ran about and shouted while women cried or fainted. But a twelve-year-old boy known as the "water rat" pushed his way through the crowd, jumped into the river and followed the girl beneath the ice. He managed to grab her hand and pull her across open water to the edge of the ice, where another Dutch girl pulled them out. Men onshore brought planks and used them to cross the gap and then wrapped the unconscious girl in blankets and took her home.

The lad refused offers of help, waded to shore and walked to a nearby blacksmith shop. Wrapped in a horse blanket while his clothes were drying, he was surrounded by a crowd of admirers, and an Irish lady brought him a pan of hot soup. He had made his own skates by grinding down old mill files, but a shopkeeper who had several skates on the shelves of his store had a pair sent to the boy as a reward.

## THE BRANDED HAND

Though Jonathan Walker has been dead for more than 130 years, his right hand is still held high. Carved in granite at the top of a ten-foot monument at his grave in Muskegon's Evergreen Cemetery, the hand with a branded double "S" was the subject of one of John Greenleaf Whittier's stirring antislavery poems.

Walker's hand was branded in 1844 after his conviction in Florida on a charge of slave stealing. In an effort to help seven slaves gain their freedom, he took them aboard his ship at Pensacola and headed toward the Bahamas. However, he was incapacitated by severe sunstroke, and the others aboard were unable to navigate the boat. Rescued by a wrecking sloop, they were taken to Key West and then Pensacola, where Walker was imprisoned.

Tried and convicted, he was condemned to the pillory, where he was the target of rotten eggs thrown by George Willis, one of the owners of the slaves, and other local citizens. When the "SS" (signifying "slave stealer") was burned into his palm, he became the only person ever to have been branded by order of a federal court.

In describing the experience later, Walker wrote that the branding iron was pressed against his hand and held firmly for fifteen or twenty seconds. "It made a spattering noise," he said, "like a handful of salt in the fire, as the skin seared and gave way to the hot iron. The pain was severe while the iron was on, and for some time afterwards."

Walker was imprisoned and released only after eleven months when northern abolitionists paid $596.05 for his fine and costs.

Punishment for aiding the slaves was not the first distress Walker encountered. At the age of fifteen, he fell through ice on a frozen pond and nearly perished. When he was seventeen, he began sailing and soon, after becoming ill in the Indian Ocean, was put ashore among strangers who didn't share his language. He recovered after twenty days and returned to familiar shores. Less than a year later, a fierce gale in the English Channel

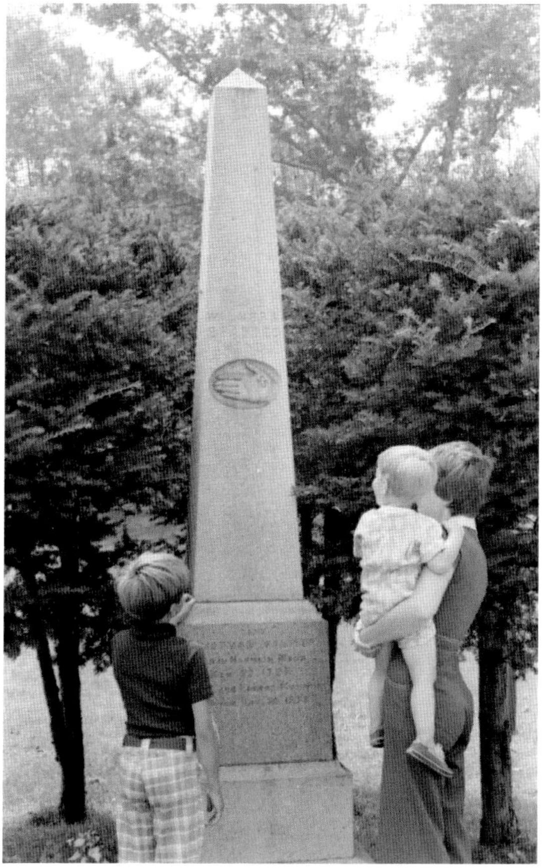

At Evergreen Cemetery in Muskegon, a mother tells her sons about Jonathan Walker and his branded hand, subjects of a poem by John Greenleaf Whittier. Walker, an abolitionist who helped slaves to gain freedom, is the only person ever branded by order of a federal court. *Author's collection.*

knocked him senseless to the deck of his ship. After about another year, during a voyage from Europe to the United States, another gale blew him from atop a yardarm into the ocean during the dead of night. Luckily, he caught hold of a dangling rope and eventually was pulled to safety. Five years later, he contracted yellow fever during an epidemic in Havana but again survived.

About a decade later, he began correspondence with Benjamin Lundy, lecturer and publisher of an antislavery newspaper. With his twelve-year-old son and another youth, Walker sailed to Metamoras, Mexico, to see the 138,000 acres that the Mexican government had given Lundy to establish a colony for freed slaves.

From there, the trio made several chartered voyages back to New Orleans, carrying business correspondence. When they reached shore in Mexico on the last trip, they were attacked by robbers. Walker's son ran back into the sea, and the other young man tried to escape but was captured. Walker was shot twice, in a wrist and the abdomen, but he managed to get into the water and swim away despite bleeding profusely and being unable to use the arm with the wounded wrist. When it became dark, the father and son were able to make it safely to shore.

For five years after his release from the jail in Pensacola, Walker lectured against slavery. He came to Muskegon in about 1850. In 1863, he purchased a few acres at the west end of Mona Lake, where he raised fruit until his death in 1878.

On the base of the monument at his grave is engraved one of the verses of Whittier's poem, "The Branded Hand":

*Then lift that manly right hand*
*Bold ploughman of the wave!*
*Its branded palm shall testify*
*Salvation to the slave!*
*Hold up its fire-wrought language*
*That those who read may feel*
*His heart swell strong within him,*
*His sinews change to steal.*

## Keepers of the Peace

Long before the days of patrol cars, law violators in Grand Rapids were marched off to the city jail on foot or, if they were too inebriated to walk, were transported in wheelbarrows.

Those single-wheel vehicles saw plenty of action during the nineteenth century, when lumberjacks frequented the town's more than two hundred saloons and passed out from overdoses or from punches in the nightly street brawls.

The first enforcers of the law were the mayor and councilmen, who had authority to make arrests and settle disputes. In 1856, midtown merchants hired Henry Baker to patrol Canal and Monroe Avenues between Lyon and Ottawa Streets, and a year later revision of the city charter enabled the common council to appoint a constable and a watchman for each ward.

Establishment of the first regular police force came in 1871 with the hiring of eight patrolmen and appointment of James L. Moran as chief.

Since that time, thousands of the city's finest citizens have joined the ranks of the Grand Rapids Police Department. For the first three-quarters of a century, all were men—except for a nonuniformed matron on the staff as early as the late 1800s. The first female officer was Betty Koster, who joined the department in 1946 after service during World War II in the U.S. Navy's Women Accepted for Volunteer Emergency Service (WAVES).

Walter W. Coe, World War I veteran and local baseball star, became the city's first black policeman in 1922. He was regarded as one of the department's most capable members and eventually attained the rank of captain. Coe died at his desk at police headquarters after thirty-five years with the department.

The Grand Rapids force has grown to have more than 330 uniformed personnel and about 100 civilian employees today. Wheelbarrows were replaced by horse-drawn patrol wagons and eventually by motorized vehicles. Procedures used to identify criminals have improved. Grand Rapids police in 1897 adopted the Bertillon system of identification, which involved measurements, followed by fingerprinting and, more recently, DNA typing.

Before the end of the nineteenth century, a police signal system was installed, with call boxes at several locations in the central city. Patrolmen used them to report to headquarters and, if necessary, summon a patrol wagon, a conveyance pulled by two horses that responded not only to alarms called in by the officers but also to those phoned in by private citizens.

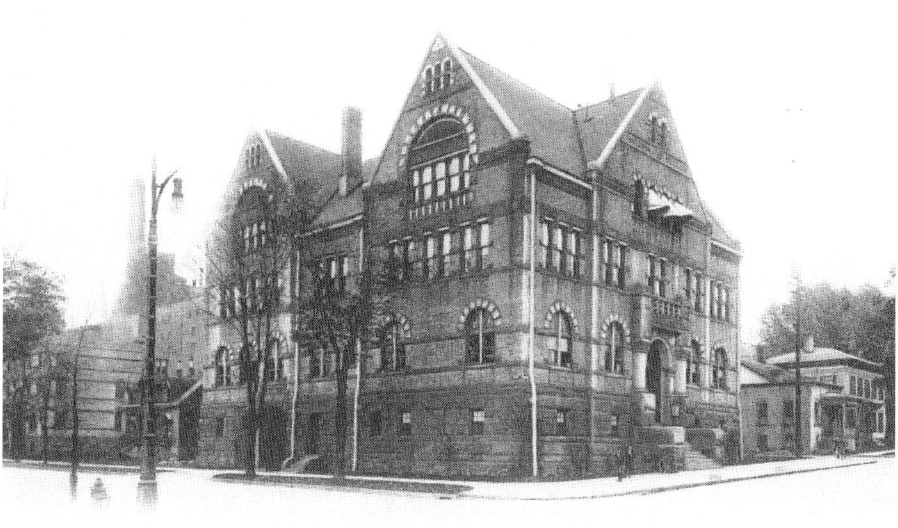

Constructed at the corner of Crescent Street and Ottawa Avenue in 1892, this building served as police headquarters for more than seventy years. Operations were then moved to the corner of Monroe Avenue and Michigan Street for thirty-five years before shifting to the department's present location at Division Avenue and Monroe Center.

With a top speed of thirty-five miles per hour, the department's first motorized patrol vehicle arrived in 1911. Two years later, three automobiles and three motorcycles joined it to end the horse era, and two souped-up motorcycles were added the next year.

The city's first police headquarters was located on the second floor of a grocery store at the corner of Monroe and Ionia, and in 1882 the department was moved to Lyon and Campau, where it remained for ten years. A new four-story headquarters, constructed in 1892 at Crescent and Ottawa, became the center of the city's police activity until 1966, when it was moved to another new building adjacent to the Hall of Justice at the corner of Monroe and Michigan.

In 2001, officers moved into the present police station bounded by Monroe, Division and Fulton—a building that had been a shopper's delight after its opening in 1949 as the home of Herpolsheimer's Department Store.

## Saddlebag Swamp

In the daytime it was pleasant. At night it was scary. On one occasion it was hungry. And now it's gone.

To Grand Rapids area pioneers, it was known as Saddlebag Swamp, a name derived from its shape, looking much like the twin bags that were slung across the backs of horses behind their saddles. The soggy terrain of several hundred acres was located just beyond the southeast corner of today's Meijer Gardens and Sculpture Park. Soon after settlers from the east moved into the area, the swamp was a popular destination for wildflower admirers in the spring, berry pickers in the summer and hunters during autumn.

In the dark, however, the area was best crossed with caution. An early volume of Kent County history tells of the experience of a doctor returning from a house call and passing the swamp at midnight. "As he was meditating on his home and a bed," the book notes, "the horse became frightened, shied at a huge panther which crossed the trail and tossed the man of medicine from the saddle."

During daylight, the principal threats were snakes, according to Grand Rapids mayor and congressman Charles Belknap. He recalled in his book (*The Yesterdays of Grand Rapids*) that when wildflower lovers went to the swamp, many wore hip boots "more as a protection against snakes than water, for everything in the line of wiggling serpents, from the harmless little garter snakes to the black water snakes, rattlers, and blue racers might be encountered there."

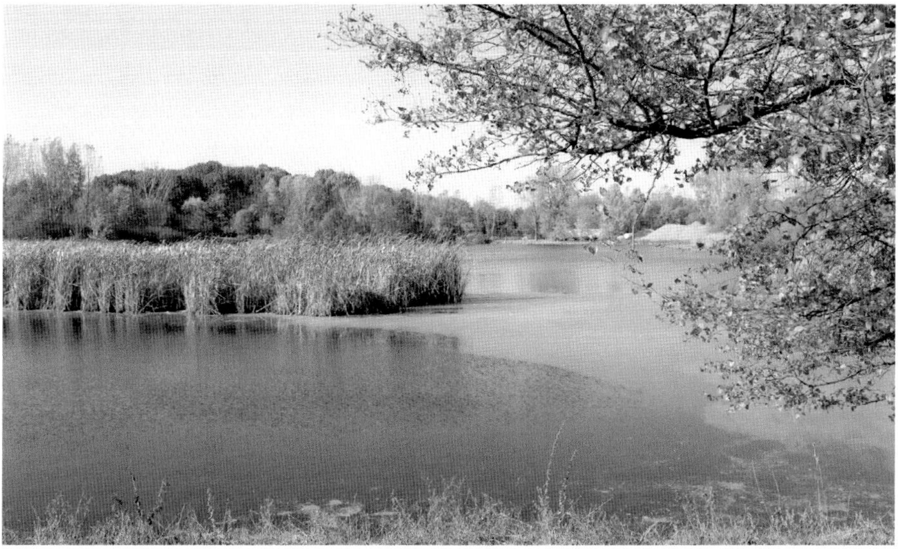

In the mid-nineteenth century Saddlebag Swamp was a popular gathering place for Grand Rapids–area berry pickers. But when builders of the first railroad to the area reached wetlands east of the city in 1858, the swamp demonstrated that it, too, had an appetite. One night it swallowed a construction train that sank sixty feet into an underground lake. *Author's collection.*

Berry picking at the swamp once enabled Belknap to enjoy a memorable Independence Day during his childhood. Going downtown for the parade, fireworks and other festivities would require a bit of money, but he had none. His mother suggested that he go to the swamp and pick berries to sell. "I fought snakes and worked until dark," he said, "but I got enough ripe berries to fill the basket and my hat." He sold the berries to the cook at the National Hotel and enjoyed an especially happy holiday.

In 1858, the swamp's gluttonous appetite became apparent to crews laying track for the Detroit and Milwaukee Railroad, which would soon give Grand Rapids residents their first taste of travel by rail. As they moved westward from Detroit and reached the edge of Grand Rapids Township, the workers began to place rails through the Saddlebag area. However, when they came to work one morning, they were astounded to discover that the swamp had swallowed the locomotive and cars of their construction train.

The equipment and a section of track had sunk out of sight into an underground lake sixty feet below ground level. The company then decided to alter the route, according to historian Arthur Scott White, and the rails were laid in a half circle around the swamp. The curves were sharp and the route change was costly.

## Out of Steam

Soon after the Detroit and Milwaukee's first locomotive chugged into Grand Rapids in 1858, the line was carrying passengers to and from the city's first depot, just north of today's Belknap Park. It wasn't an impressive building at just fifty by twenty-four feet; here, according to local politician and author Charles Belknap, "men hovered over the old heater stove and used the floor for a cuspidor while the women curled up disconsolately on the wooden benches."

Before development of a streetcar route in 1865, passengers from downtown had to take buggies or walk two miles on dirt roads between the central city and the Leonard-Plainfield area.

Grand Rapids had several other depots through the years, the grandest of which was Union Depot, which was completed in 1900 at Ionia Avenue at Oakes Street. By 1905, 1,000 persons a day were boarding trains there. That year, twenty-thousand trains and 750,000 passengers made it a busy hub at the heart of the city. During World Wars I and II, it was the site of many sad farewells and joyous welcomes for servicemen and their families and sweethearts.

Alongside the building was a huge shed, 600 by 150 feet, which sheltered passengers as they walked between the trains and the station. In 1961, it was razed to clear the way for US-131 freeway construction. But half of it lived again when it was disassembled, moved south and reconstructed for use as a timber storage warehouse at the VKW Hardwoods complex on Fifty-fourth Street. An early morning fire in 2004 reduced the old structure to ashes. The other half of the shed, parts of which were stored nearby, was not damaged.

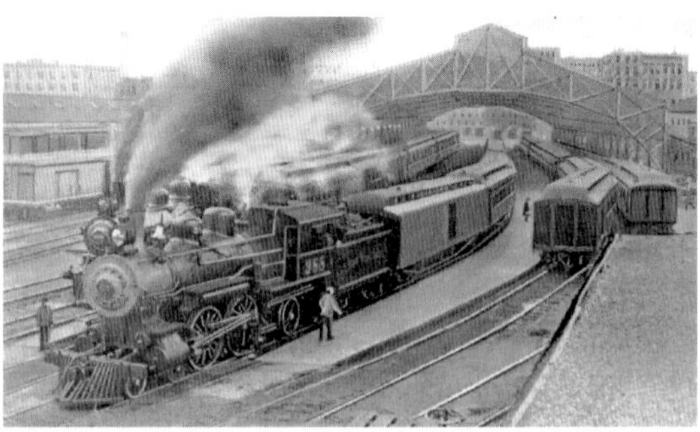

The thousands of passengers who arrived and departed from Union Depot on Ionia Avenue at Oakes Street were protected by a six-hundred- by one-hundred-foot shed that covered the tracks. Removed in 1961 to make way for the US-131 Freeway, half of it was reassembled to provide storage for lumber at a Fifty-fourth Street business. But it was leveled by fire in 2004.

Today, of course, steam trains are a rarity. Few persons other than old-timers remember the sounds of those whistles in the distance or the thundering, hissing, clanking locomotives as they roared past.

You can still see, though not hear, one at Grand Haven, where a four-hundred-ton Berkshire locomotive of the Pere Marquette Railroad rests. It's at Jackson and Second Streets in what once was the terminal yard of the Detroit, Grand Haven and Milwaukee Railway.

And you can hear one if you watch the 2004 movie *Polar Express*. Chris Van Allsburg, author of the story on which the film was based, grew up in Grand Rapids and was inspired to write the book by his memories of haunting whistles and train rides with his father.

As the tracks continued to extend westward, Grand Rapids residents first heard the sound of a locomotive whistle on June 27, 1858, when a construction train neared the northeastern edge of the city. Less than a week later, on July 2, the locomotive *Empire* steamed past the station just south of the junction of Leonard Street and Plainfield Avenue and continued on to a dock on the river at Pearl Street. Then it was carried across the stream on a scow and placed on rails being extended to Grand Haven.

Regular service between Grand Rapids and Detroit began on July 13, and according to historian Albert Baxter, newspapers pointed out that local residents "for the first time could leave their homes by a conveyance other than river steamer or stage coach." The first train to make the trip from Detroit to Grand Haven passed through Grand Rapids on September 1.

Trains finally were able to cross Saddlebag Swamp about twenty years later when the route was changed again after the sixty-foot-deep morass was filled with sand, gravel and timbers.

## Kissing Bridges

Inside two old covered bridges straddling the Flat River, about a dozen miles east of Grand Rapids, are weathered wooden boards with clues to a big part of the romantic history of the surrounding area.

For nearly a century and a half, young lovers have whittled their initials on the siding and support timbers of Fallasburg Bridge (at the east edge of Kent County) and White's Bridge (just a few miles away in Ionia County).

A few generations ago, these spans and others like them provided veils of privacy for courting couples that reined in horses and halted buggies to enjoy secluded togetherness inside the roofed structures. They were known as kissing bridges then, and for good reason.

The village of Ada has a well-known span that crosses the Thornapple River, but it is a replica. The original bridge stood at the site for more than one hundred years before its roof collapsed under heavy snow early in 1979. It was quickly repaired but then was obliterated by arsonists before the end of that year. Had it not been destroyed by fire, the 125-foot-long Ada Bridge, built in 1867, would he considered Michigan's oldest covered bridge.

Instead, the 117-foot-long White's Bridge in Ionia County is, without challenge, the oldest in the state. A historical marker notes that it was built in 1867, though most sources claim that it was completed in 1869—since payment for construction was made in 1870. The Fallasburg Bridge, 100 feet in length, was constructed in 1871.

The third of Michigan's original covered bridges still standing is Langley Bridge over the St. Joseph River at Centreville near the Indiana border. Built in 1887, it's the state's longest at 282 feet.

Before its demise by fire, the span at Ada was threatened several times by water. When the river was at flood stage, siding was sometimes removed to permit water to pass through. And farmers are said to have driven wagonloads of rock onto the bridge to help keep it from being swept away.

The rebuilt Ada bridge, which was opened in 1980, is not open to vehicular traffic. White's and Fallasburg Bridges still accommodate automobiles, but signs above entrances at Fallasburg warn that there's a "$5 fine for riding or driving on this bridge faster than a walk."

To tour the three nearest covered bridges from downtown Grand Rapids, take Interstate 96 east to the M-21 exit. Follow M-21 east to the edge of Ada and turn south at the light onto Bronson Street, which leads to the replicated bridge. From Ada, take M-21 east to Lowell. Turn north on Hudson Street, which becomes Lake Avenue, and then turn east on Fallasburg County Park Road and follow the signs to Fallasburg Park and Fallasburg Bridge. From the bridge at Fallasburg, drive northeast on Covered Bridge Road. Turn east on McPherson Street, which becomes Potters Road in Ionia County, and then go north on White's Bridge Road and proceed to White's Bridge.

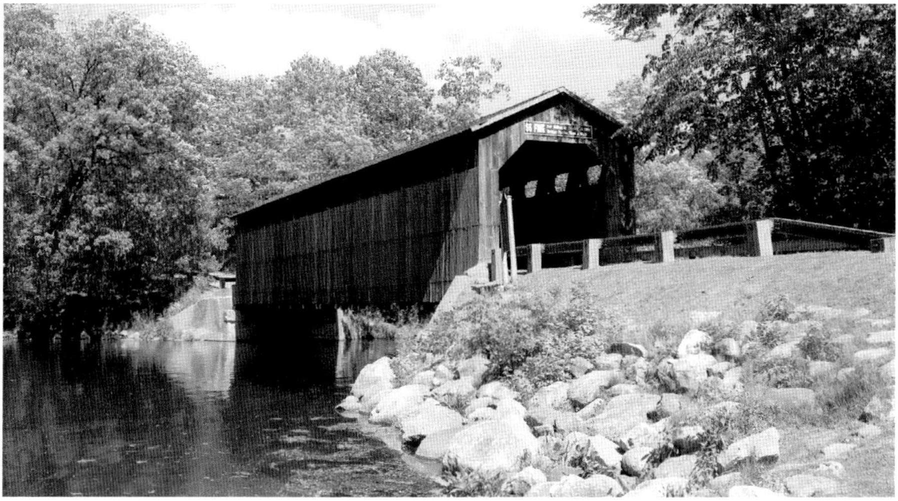

Two of the three ancient covered bridges still standing in Michigan are within about a mile of each other near Lowell in eastern Kent County. This one is Fallasburg Bridge, which spans Flat River in Fallasburg Park, a popular picnic site for Grand Rapids–area residents. Just a few miles away in Ionia County is White's Bridge. The state's third surviving covered bridge is at Centreville near the Indiana border. *Author's collection.*

If this tour whets your appetite for more old bridges, head south into Indiana and visit Parke County (west of Indianapolis at the Illinois border), where water still flows beneath more than thirty of the old covered spans.

## Our Women's Role in the Civil War

When the men of Grand Rapids marched off to save the Union a century and a half ago, the city's women wiped away tears and prepared to take on a greater share of family responsibilities. There would now be no brothers or sons to help with chores and no fathers to assist with maintenance of the house and care of the children.

Still, the ladies were determined to help with the war effort. Just ten days after the conflict began, they met in Mills and Clancy's Hall on Canal Street (now Lower Monroe Avenue) to form the Soldiers' Aid Society. Two days later they started bringing in sewing kits and bandages for soldiers of the Third Michigan Infantry Regiment at Cantonment Anderson, a temporary camp located on the old fairgrounds at Jefferson Avenue and Hall Street.

The site is now marked by a large boulder at the campus of the Gerald R. Ford Job Corps Center (formerly South High School).

Another of the society's first goals was to provide the regiment with a suitable banner. The women decided that one side of the flag would contain the arms of the United States, with the words "Volunteers, Third Regiment, Mich." On the other side would be the same arms, with the inscription "The Ladies of Grand Rapids to the Third Regiment Michigan Infantry."

The banner was stitched by Miss Mattie Ferguson; on June 4, 1861, it was delivered to the camp by thirty-four ladies, one for each state. The women wore blue dresses with red and white sashes, and each carried a blue parasol with thirteen gold stars. Marching behind the carriages that took them to the camp were a large crowd, a brass band and a glee club.

Miss Rebecca Richmond, daughter of Grand Rapids pioneers William A. and Lorraine Richmond, was one of the young women who presented the banner to officers of the regiment. In a journal that she kept during the first two years of the war, she recorded her thoughts about events in the city and

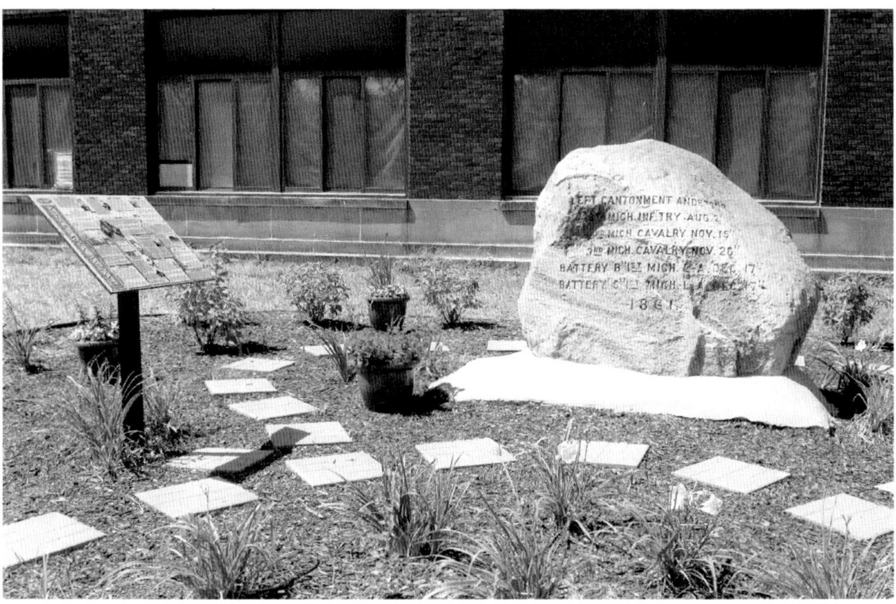


Here on the campus of what was South High School and now is the Gerald R. Ford Job Corps Center, a large boulder and display panel remind visitors that Grand Rapids soldiers of the Third Michigan Infantry Regiment assembled there and prepared themselves for Civil War action. A temporary camp known as Cantonment Anderson, it previously was the city fairgrounds. *Author's collection.*

action on the battlefields. In her entry for June 13, 1861, she wrote: "One of the saddest days in the record of Grand Rapids. Our pet regiment, the Third, has departed at last and left many, many sorrowing hearts behind. They started from Cantonment Anderson at about 8 o'clock accompanied by a vast procession of carriages. Their march through the city to the depot at Plainfield Avenue and Leonard Street was a continual ovation. The Star-Spangled banner floated over them from almost every building along the route, handkerchiefs waved from thousands of fair hands, and young girls showered the troops with bouquets."

She said that several of the girls picked large leaves as mementoes and attached labels with the date of the departure and a quote from "Kathleen Mavourneen," a popular song of the time: "It may be for years, and it may be forever."

The banner that Mattie Ferguson sewed was carried into many of the Third Regiment's battles, and on May 31, 1862, at the Battle of Fair Oaks in Virginia, it was in the hands of Sergeant Charles Foster, the first Union army volunteer from Lansing. He carried it through several charges until a bullet hit him in the neck. As he fell, he gripped the staff firmly and shouted, "Don't let the colors go down!" The banner was rescued by Ezra Ransome of Shiawassee County and continued to inspire soldiers of the regiment until March 1863, when it was returned to Grand Rapids.

Though tattered and torn, it was displayed at regimental reunions and carried in parades until 1882, when it was sent to join other battle flags at the state capitol. Sadly, Mattie Ferguson never heard about how greatly her banner inspired Third Regiment soldiers as they rushed into battle. She died of tuberculosis two weeks after she created it.

## Saluting the *Monitor*'s Commander

Just four months after he was partially blinded in the first combat between ironclad ships, John Lorimer Worden was in Grand Rapids, visiting his mother and receiving accolades at a ceremony in his honor at Luce's Hall on Monroe Avenue.

The Civil War had been raging little more than a year when, on March 9, 1862, the USS *Monitor*, with Worden in command, battled the CSS *Virginia*, a ship that the Confederate States of America rebuilt from the sunken remains of the USS *Merrimack*. Although both sides claimed victory, the battle was inconclusive. However, the conflict did signal the obsolescence of wooden warships.

During the conflict, Worden was peering through a port in the turret when a Confederate shell hit the ship and drove powder and metal fragments into his face. While recuperating in Washington, D.C., he was visited by President Abraham Lincoln; shortly after that, he accompanied the president to Washington Navy Yard, where they inspected the *Monitor*.

Earlier in the Civil War, Worden had the dubious distinction of becoming the conflict's first prisoner of war when he was captured by Confederates after delivering secret orders to the Federal fleet at Pensacola. He was held for seven months before being released in a prisoner exchange. After the war, he continued in the navy and served as superintendent of the Naval Academy from 1869 to 1872.

On July 9, 1862, according to news reports, Luce's Hall "was literally packed with patriots of all classes, ages and sexes, who had come to see and extend a hand of welcome and a hearty greeting to the patriot and hero." Local dignitaries and Worden himself addressed the crowd during the program, which also included patriotic songs with solos by Cora Bliss

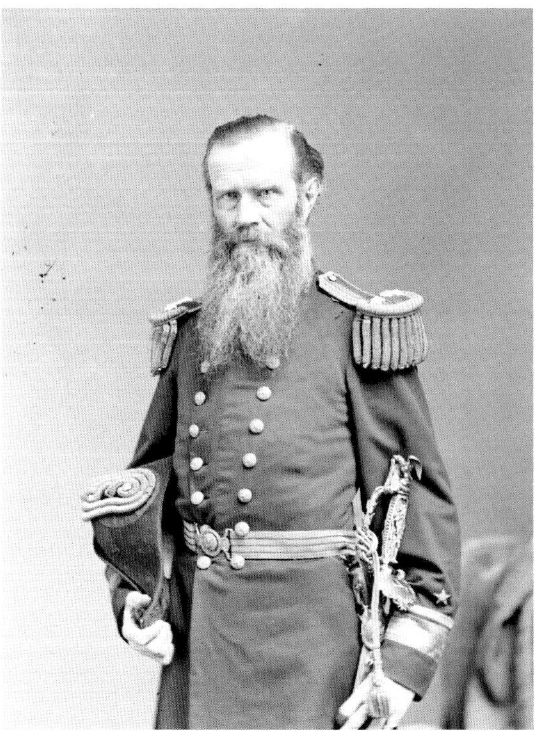

Shortly after commanding the USS *Monitor* in the first battle between ironclad warships, John Lorimer Worden visited family members and accepted the praise of friends and patriots at a ceremony in a downtown Grand Rapids assembly hall. *Courtesy of Library of Congress.*

Wenham, a soprano in the St. Mark's Episcopal Church choir. She was accompanied by Mary E. Stuart Church, the organist at St. Mark's.

The climax of the event was what one report called "a bevy of beauty and loveliness"—thirty young women who encircled the naval hero, throwing bouquets at his feet and singing three songs composed especially for the occasion.

Most likely, those in the crowd included Worden's mother (Harriet Graham Worden), as well as several siblings and other relatives. His father, Ananias Worden Sr., two of his brothers and a sister were no longer living. Two other brothers probably were not at the celebration. Frederick W., an officer in the Union army, most likely was fighting in the South. Ananias Jr. was at that time in Chicago, where he was co-owner and business manager of the *Chicago Times*.

The younger Ananias apparently didn't share the patriotic fervor of his older brothers. During his tenure at the *Times* (1861–65), the paper sided with the Copperheads, a group of Northern Democrats who opposed the war and advocated an immediate peace settlement. One *Times* editorial tirade in 1863 prompted Union general Ambrose Burnside to order the paper to cease publication. When Ananias and principal owner Roger Storey ignored the decree, soldiers invaded the pressroom and enforced it. But two days later, Lincoln rescinded the order.

Ananias Worden Sr. brought most of his family from New York State to Michigan in the 1840s. Early histories of Montcalm County mention Frederick W. and Ananias being at what is now the village of Gowen as early as 1844. Ananias was elected to the Michigan legislature in 1848, but it is unclear whether this was the elder or younger Ananias. Frederick W. was the first supervisor of Montcalm Township, then part of Ionia County, in 1845 and was succeeded by Ananias in 1846.

The histories mention no other members of the Worden family, and those who were in Montcalm apparently soon moved southeast to Kent County's Courtland Township, where Frederick W. was supervisor in 1850. Ananias Sr. owned a large tract of land at the south edge of the township, along today's 10 Mile Road between Meyer's Lake Avenue and Brower Lake. Ananias Jr. had a farm directly across the road in Cannon Township.

Today, the only visible traces of the family are weathered old grave markers at Courtland Cemetery, two miles north of the sites of the family farms.

## BEEN THERE, DONE THAT

Today's talk of streetcars cruising through downtown Grand Rapids may be exciting, but it's nothing new. Nearly a century and a half ago, trolleys began carrying passengers through the central city between the railroad depot at Plainfield Avenue and Leonard Street and the east end of the line at Jefferson Avenue and Fulton Street.

Most of the route was along Monroe Avenue, and the cars were pulled by horses. Free rides introduced residents to the new means of travel on the line's first day of operation, May 10, 1865. On following days, the fare was limited to five cents and the speed to six miles per hour by city council regulations.

Today, planners envision a three-mile system through the central city between the Sixth Street Bridge and the Rapid Central Station. They predict that future expansion might bring lines to Eastown and East Grand Rapids, to the downtown campus of Grand Valley State University and to the north on Plainfield Avenue.

The city's comparatively short route of the 1860s sprouted into a system of more than thirty-one miles of double track in the early decades of the twentieth century. Along with the additional track came many improvements in operation. In the 1870s, additional companies began providing service, one carrying passengers between downtown and the old fairgrounds at Hall Street and Jefferson Avenue and another running out to the pavilion and picnic grounds at Reeds Lake.

The pioneer lines offered convenience, but comfort was absent. Cars without springs made rides rough, and frequent derailments required assistance from passengers to put the vehicles back on the tracks. In addition, strap rails—metal strips attached to wooden beams—became hazardous when the strips broke loose, curling upward and penetrating floors of cars.

In 1877, the Reeds Lake line replaced horses with a large steam locomotive that could pull three passenger cars along the route known as the "dummy line." The noisy steam engines irritated nearby residents, and during an early 1900s riot, the tracks were torn up.

In response to requests for service in the Michigan and Lyon Street hill district, a cable car line began operation in 1888, patterned after the San Francisco system established in 1873. Eventually, consolidation of the city's various lines and replacement of horses, steam engines and cables with electricity as the power source brought improved service.

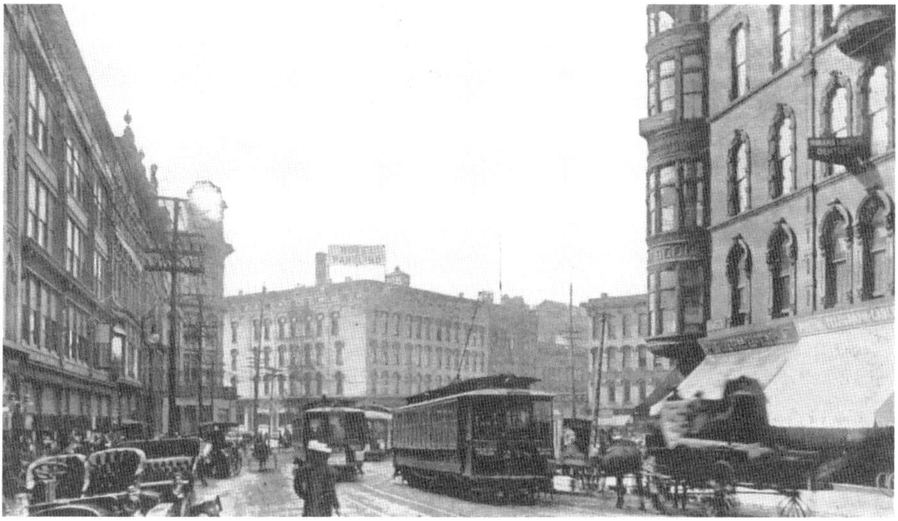

During the early days of downtown streetcar operations, trolleys competed with horses and buggies for space on Monroe Avenue near Campau Square. By the 1930s, patronage had declined, and tracks throughout the city were torn up.

In 1900, new owners of the system hired L.J. DeLamarter to manage the company's North Park and Ramona Park resorts. A promoter extraordinaire, DeLamarter added new attractions to the parks that thrived. By 1920 he had become vice-president and general manager of the streetcar system.

His door-to-door surveys to get feedback on streetcar operation and his policy of responding to all customer complaints resulted in greater patronage. To ease concerns about safety, he had attractive young women ride atop streetcars with banners proclaiming, "Don't Worry—Relax! Ride the streetcar. It's the safest place in town."

When a fire at the Hall Street car barn destroyed fifty-seven of the company's streetcars in 1925, DeLamarter proposed new cars half as heavy as the old ones and using roller bearings on wheels. His improved design set the standard for streetcars throughout the country.

In disposing of the remaining older cars, DeLamarter staged a grand show at the West Michigan Fairgrounds with a balloon ascension and fireworks. Then, a string of twenty of the old cars, filled with kerosene-soaked hay and gunpowder, was torched. The spectacular blaze could be seen for miles.

Despite such theatrics, declining patronage during the Great Depression forced the company into receivership in the early 1930s, and the end of the city's first streetcar era came on August 23, 1935, with a final run on the Cherry-Plainfield route.

## Just Happy Memories Remain

For more than a century, the shores of Reeds Lake attracted throngs from Grand Rapids seeking fresh air and fun. By the mid-1800s, picnic groves had combined with the lake's ideal waters for fishing and swimming to entice good-time seekers who came on foot and in horse-drawn buggies.

Horse-pulled trolleys on light rails began carrying passengers to the lake in 1875, and a few years later a steam locomotive replaced the horses. By the end of the century, the lines had been electrified, and the trolley company boasted that patrons could get "a trolley car ride of 21 miles, visit three parks, and see a vaudeville show for twenty cents." The cars went through John Ball Park and North Park on the way to Reeds Lake.

In 1894, the Grand Rapids Street Railway Company began developing a recreational facility on the lake that would increase its patronage. Streetcar companies throughout the country were also connecting with "trolley parks." Unlike many of those, the one at Reeds Lake enabled streetcars to carry patrons directly into the park, and there was no charge for admission. This free-gate policy continued throughout the park's existence.

When a new theater was built in 1897, replacing an earlier one destroyed by fire, the company held a contest to name it. "Ramona" was the winning

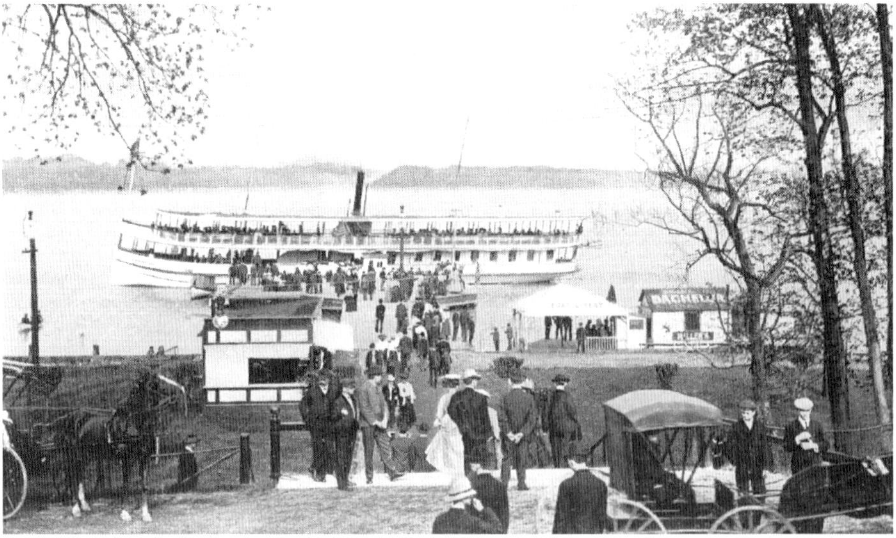

For more than a century, big-name entertainers and big-league baseball teams lured fun-lovers to Ramona Park at the shore of Reeds Lake in East Grand Rapids. Others were attracted by the park's many attractions and rides, such as those on the steamboats that cruised the lake for seven decades.

entry, and as other structures were added, it became the designation for the entire complex.

The theater presented programs by a variety of celebrities, including Carrie Nation of the Woman's Christian Temperance Union and comedienne and Ziegfeld Follies star Fanny Brice. Among others who took the stage throughout the years were Will Rogers, the Marx Brothers, Jimmy Durante, Edgar Bergen, Danny Kaye, Jack Benny and Fred Allen.

Ramona Gardens, a dance hall, was built nearby in the early 1900s and featured the big bands of Glenn Miller, Tommy Dorsey, Bob Crosby, Shep Fields, Glen Gray, Ted Weems and Anson Weeks.

In 1903 about four thousand fans were on hand to see the Detroit Tigers defeat the Washington Senators in an exhibition game at a field opposite the park on Wealthy Street. Later that year, the Street Railway Company bought the field and built the larger Ramona Athletic Park, which attracted major-league teams such as the Cincinnati Reds, Philadelphia Athletics, St. Louis Cardinals and New York Yankees. Babe Ruth hit two home runs there in 1928. Today, the site is home field for East Grand Rapids High School's football teams.

Among popular attractions added to Ramona Park throughout the years was a roller coaster, first named the Derby Racer and then the Jack Rabbit. The double-track ride with an eighty-foot dip was claimed to be the steepest, fastest and safest in the country.

Young children rode the prancing horses on a huge carousel, with musical accompaniment provided by three band organs: Sadie Mae, Madame Laura and Big Bertha. Their music can still he heard and purchased online.

Children, and many adults, also rode through the park on a miniature train pulled by a real steam locomotive—not an electric-powered replica like those at most other entertainment complexes. When Ramona eventually closed, the train operated for a time at Lowell before being moved to Burley Park near Howard City where it carries passengers about five weekends each summer.

Other Ramona attractions included the Mystic Chute, which took boat riders through a long, dark tunnel; bumper cars; a rifle range; and a variety of other games and concessions. But few visitors to Ramona left for home without riding on one of the steamboats that chugged around Reeds Lake. Best known were those operated by John Poisson; the first was the fifty-four-foot *Florence*, which came to the lake from Frankfurt in the 1880s.

After adding the *Victor* and the *Sport* to his fleet, Poisson introduced the 450-passenger, 130-foot *Major Watson* in 1891. In 1905, he bought the *Hazel*

*A.*, a competing watercraft that had sunk, and raised it. Both the *Major Watson* and the *Hazel A.* continued to sail the lake into the 1920s. The last Poisson steamer was the *Ramona*, a 100-foot, 435-passenger boat that started service in 1923 and sailed for more than thirty years.

When streetcars were eliminated in Grand Rapids in the 1930s and automobiles began carrying fun-seekers to more distant sites, patronage of Ramona dwindled, and its features began to disappear. Ramona Athletic Park was torn down in 1943, and the theater was razed in 1949. Then, in the mid-1950s, the entire park was sold to investors who planned to construct a shopping center and apartment complex at the site. Wrecking balls soon wiped out everything except memories of happier days at Ramona and Reeds Lake.

## A LUCKY LARD SPILL

Problems in the kitchen don't usually lead to happy endings, but one did back in the late 1800s at the home of Emma and Charles Leonard in midtown Grand Rapids. And the unlikely result was one of the largest industrial complexes ever in the metropolitan area.

Back in those days, before electrical refrigeration, huge blocks of ice were the cooling agents for keeping food fresh. One day, an enterprising maid in the Leonard household decided that she'd use the ice to quickly cool a pail of hot lard. So she set the pail atop the ice in the refrigerator and forgot about it. The ice melted beneath the hot pail, causing the pail to tip and send a stream of lard to the bottom of the refrigerator, where it solidified and clogged the drain. As Charles Leonard struggled to clean up the mess, he determined that he could build a better icebox.

The result was the Leonard Cleanable Refrigerator, which he patented and started assembling in 1881 on the second floor of a crockery store that he operated with his father and two brothers. An immediate and constantly growing success, the refrigerator enterprise demanded more and more of Leonard's time, as well as a larger space for production. During the next quarter century, operations were moved five times to various buildings in central Grand Rapids. In 1906, the firm—then known as the Grand Rapids Refrigerator Company—began making cabinets with porcelain-lined interiors, which resulted in exploding demand and a need for still more manufacturing space.

Leonard found a suitable site at the edge of the city limits on Clyde Park Avenue, just south of Grandville Avenue. In 1907, he built what

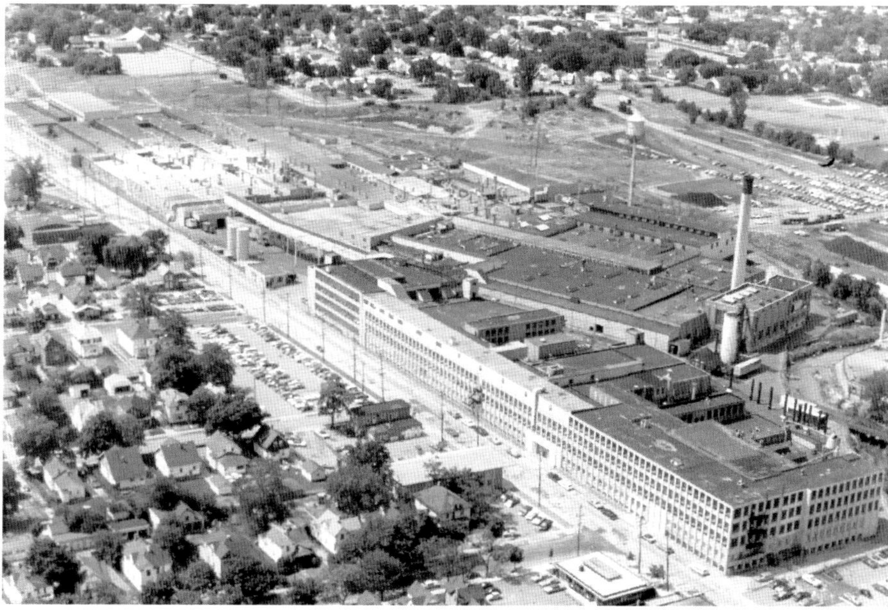

When Charles Leonard moved his refrigerator manufacturing operations to this new factory at the western city limits in 1907, it was described as the largest and most complete plant of its kind in the world. Through the years, the complex was expanded, and by the 1950s there were eighty-six buildings for the production of a wide variety of appliances.

was described in the *Grand Rapids Furniture Record* of November 1908 as "the immense new plant of the Grand Rapids Refrigerator Company. For the purpose intended, this is the largest and most complete plant in the world."

By 1918, the company's reputation for craftsmanship had caught the attention of the Kelvinator Corporation in Detroit, which began buying Leonard's cabinets for its electric refrigeration units. The Grand Rapids Refrigerator Company continued to be the leading manufacturer of boxes cooled with ice.

In 1926, the firm was renamed Leonard Refrigerator Company, and it was acquired by Kelvinator. Kelvinator merged with Nash Motor Company in the late 1930s to form Nash-Kelvinator Corporation, and in 1954 the largest merger in the automobile industry to date affected Grand Rapids when American Motors Corporation linked Nash-Kelvinator with Hudson Motors. By 1958, AMC concentrated its entire appliance production at the Grand Rapids factory. At that time, there were eighty-six buildings at the large industrial complex, which produced not only refrigerators but also electric ranges, washing machines, driers, freezers and ice cream cabinets.

A decade after its creation, AMC sold its Grand Rapids operation to White Consolidated Industries. A.B. Electrolux bought out WCI in 1986 and, within a year, had moved the last appliance manufacturing operations of the factory to facilities in other states.

Several parts of the complex continued to be used by various small businesses for manufacturing and storage, but the main building that Charles Leonard had constructed in 1907 was plagued by a series of fires in the 1990s; it had been razed by the end of the century.

Sadly, Leonard's pride and joy lives on only in the memories of workers who spent much of their lives within its walls. But what had started out a dark day in the Leonard kitchen more than a century earlier proved to bring good fortune for many years to the Leonards, as well as to all of Grand Rapids.

## When the Army Arrived

It has been 125 years since the Salvation Army's tiny invasion force arrived in Grand Rapids and launched a crusade to make the city a better place. Its headquarters was quickly established in late November 1883 in a rental room on Pearl Street at the site of today's Amway Grand Plaza Hotel.

The unit was the Army's first corps to be established in Michigan, and its officers were two ladies, Captain Jane McCracken and Lieutenant Jennie Hall. Their new outpost wasn't impressive. An old stove was procured to take the edge off autumn frost, and kerosene lamps were hung above seats made of boards.

The single frill was a bass drum, and that wasn't especially appreciated by many locals. It became the prime mover for noisy street processions, and its continuous thumping brought complaints to the police. On several occasions, some participants were arrested and imprisoned. After the city tried to block the parades, the Michigan Supreme Court ruled that the marchers had a constitutional right to continue without hindrance.

When the ladies arrived at the depot, wagon driver Casey De Blond delivered their only possessions, an ancient trunk and a suitcase, to the cheap lodging place that had been arranged for them. Of course, on the way he became aware that they were members of the Salvation Army, and being accustomed to consuming alcohol rather liberally, he made a quick escape to avoid chastisement—not even pausing to collect his five-cent fee.

Surprisingly, however, he showed up at the Army's first official meeting—probably out of curiosity—and became a convert, the first Salvation Army recruit in the city.

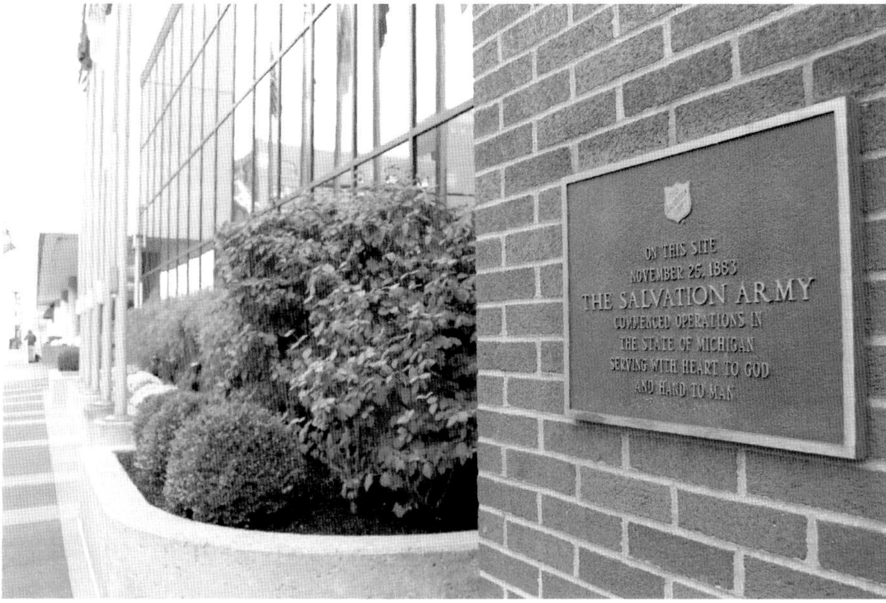


A marker on the wall of the Amway Grand Plaza Hotel in downtown Grand Rapids identifies the site of the Salvation Army's first headquarters in Michigan. Two female officers spearheaded the Army's peaceful invasion in 1883, and their first convert was an alcohol-loving wagon driver who carried their luggage when they arrived. *Author's collection.*

The Army's evangelistic outreach typically used outdoor meetings to attract prospects; a city ordinance at the time permitted marching and music on streets during the week, but not on Sunday. The soldiers, however, ignored the law and were jailed. Women in the group were released but demanded that if the men were kept in the jail, they'd stay there, too. So the services left the street and resumed in the jail, prompting officials to hasten the trial as much as possible.

Though it was a struggle for the Army to gain acceptance in the community, it is now recognized as a leading provider of services for the desolate and deprived. A big step in that direction came five years after the arrival of McCracken and Hall. That's when a home for unwed mothers, the first one in the Midwest, was opened at the corner of Pine Avenue and Second Street.

An improved facility was constructed in 1912 at the corner of Fulton Street and Fuller Avenue, where the Army's Booth Family Services operations are now based. For its dedication on October 29 of that year, General Evangeline Booth, commander of the Salvation Army in the United States, was the guest speaker.

An exceptional orator and a remarkable woman, Booth was the Army's first female general. Her parents, William and Catherine Booth, had founded the Christian Mission (later renamed the Salvation Army) in London, where she was born on Christmas Day 1865. As a child, she provided music at her father's meetings, and at the age of fifteen, she began preaching. Eventually, her impassioned sermons influenced thousands in Britain, Canada and the United States.

Named Eva at birth, she changed her name to Evangeline at the persuasion of friends. Though advised by her father never to marry, she adopted and raised four children. In 1919 President Woodrow Wilson awarded her a Distinguished Service Medal.

After the afternoon dedication ceremony at the new Grand Rapids home for unmarried mothers in 1912, an evening mass meeting at Powers Theater featured an address by General Booth. In her honor, the new facility was named the Evangeline Home.

## GONE BUT NOT FORGOTTEN

When roaring presses of the city's last every-morning newspaper, the *Grand Rapids Herald*, fell silent half a century ago, west Michigan residents lost a faithful breakfast table companion that had been with them for the better part of seven decades.

The loss of the paper was a disappointment for readers who scanned its pages through breakfast crumbs each morning to learn of world and local events. Failure to pull in adequate advertising revenue, except in its popular Sunday edition, hastened the *Herald*'s demise in the late 1950s.

In April 1958, it was bought by Booth Newspapers, which owned the *Grand Rapids Press*, a next-door neighbor and chief competitor. After a printers' strike shut down the *Herald* from late November to January, the paper survived only a few more months. Its last edition landed on doorsteps throughout west Michigan on March 29, 1959, and a few of its employees moved over to the neighboring *Press*, which until then had not published a Sunday paper.

Werner Veit, who had been managing editor of the *Herald*, headed the new Sunday staff that turned out the first Sunday edition of the *Press* on April 5 that year. A few years later, he was managing editor, then editor and finally publisher of the paper, as well as president of Booth Newspapers.

The *Herald*'s first breaths were taken on September 30, 1884, when its forerunner, the *Morning Telegram*, published its first edition. One of five

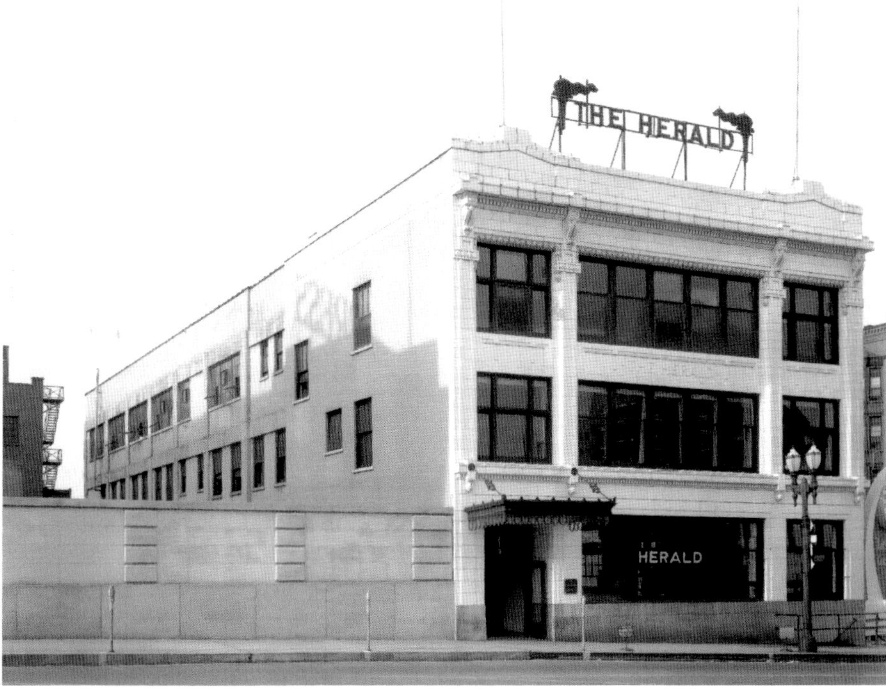


For many years, newsmen of the competing *Grand Rapids Herald* and *Grand Rapids Press* operated from adjacent buildings in the short block of Fulton Street between Division and Sheldon Avenues. But when Booth Newspapers, owner of the *Press*, bought out the *Herald* and closed it in 1959, the competition ended. Some of the *Herald*'s staff then went next door to join the ranks at the *Press*. *Courtesy of Grand Rapids History and Special Collections, Archives, Grand Rapids Public Library.*

Grand Rapids newspapers at that time, it was purchased a year and a half later by Lloyd Brezee and Fred G. Berger who combined it with the weekly *Brezee's Herald* to form the *Telegram-Herald*. That paper was the first in the city to have a female employee in the newsroom, Society Editor Etta S. Wilson. In 1888, C.G. Swensburg and Eugene D. Conger bought the *Telegram-Herald*, and in 1892, the publication's name was changed to the *Grand Rapids Herald*.

Ralph Booth of Detroit bought the *Herald* in 1905 and, a year later, sold it to William Alden Smith, who became involved in management of the paper when it was owned by Swensburg and Conger. Smith, then a congressman, later was elected to the Senate, where he was best known for heading an investigation into the sinking of the *Titanic*.

Smith was one of three men affiliated with the *Herald* at the dawn of the twentieth century who assumed prominent positions in the federal government. Arthur H. Vandenberg, selected by Smith to edit the paper, was another well-known senator. W. Franklin Knox, whose newspaper career had also begun at the *Herald*, was the unsuccessful Republican candidate for vice president in 1936 and then served as secretary of the navy in the cabinet of President Franklin D. Roosevelt, a Democrat. Almost immediately after Vandenberg left for Washington, the paper was sold to Federated Publications, a chain that also operated papers in Lansing and Battle Creek.

Until 1905, headquarters of the *Herald* was located in a building at the corner of Pearl Street and Campau Avenue, but that year operations were moved to a structure in the short block of East Fulton Street between Division and Sheldon Avenues. A year later, the *Press* was moved into its new building adjacent to the *Herald* on the corner of Fulton and Sheldon. In 1914 the *Herald* erected a new facility next to its old one, and operations continued there until the paper ceased publication. None of those structures still stand.

In the final edition of the *Herald*, a farewell editorial noted that a newspaper "does not die, as many enterprises do. It remains in yellowed clippings in family archives. It provides a history of the community in the volumes of years past, now on microfilm in the public library. The *Herald*, we hope, will be remembered as long as its youngest reader survives and as long as his descendants are interested in his life and times."

## Frank Knox Delivered

Soon after moving from Boston to Grand Rapids with his parents in 1885, eleven-year-old W. Franklin (Frank) Knox broke into the newspaper business in a big way, delivering about one hundred copies of the *Grand Rapids Democrat* in the morning, and about the same number of the *Grand Rapids Eagle* in the evening.

Fifty-five years later, after a distinguished career in newspaper publishing, he served under Franklin D. Roosevelt as secretary of the navy during World War II.

Knox dropped out of Central High School in his junior year to become a traveling salesman but eventually enrolled at Alma College. When the United States declared war on Spain in 1898, he quit school again—this time midway through his senior year in college—to join the army.

He served with Theodore Roosevelt's Rough Riders in Cuba, and that reopened the door to the newspaper world soon after his discharge and return to Grand Rapids. William Alden Smith, a congressman and president of the *Grand Rapids Herald*, was seeking reelection and hired the veteran to speak at campaign rallies and to work as a reporter at the *Herald*. Knox advanced quickly: he had been promoted to city editor before the end of 1898. A year later, he became circulation manager—back to delivery!

Knox also married his college sweetheart, Annie Reid. Their grandson is the noted actor Mark Harmon.

Hoping to have a newspaper of his own but lacking typesetting and pressroom experience, Knox consulted Grand Rapids printer John A.

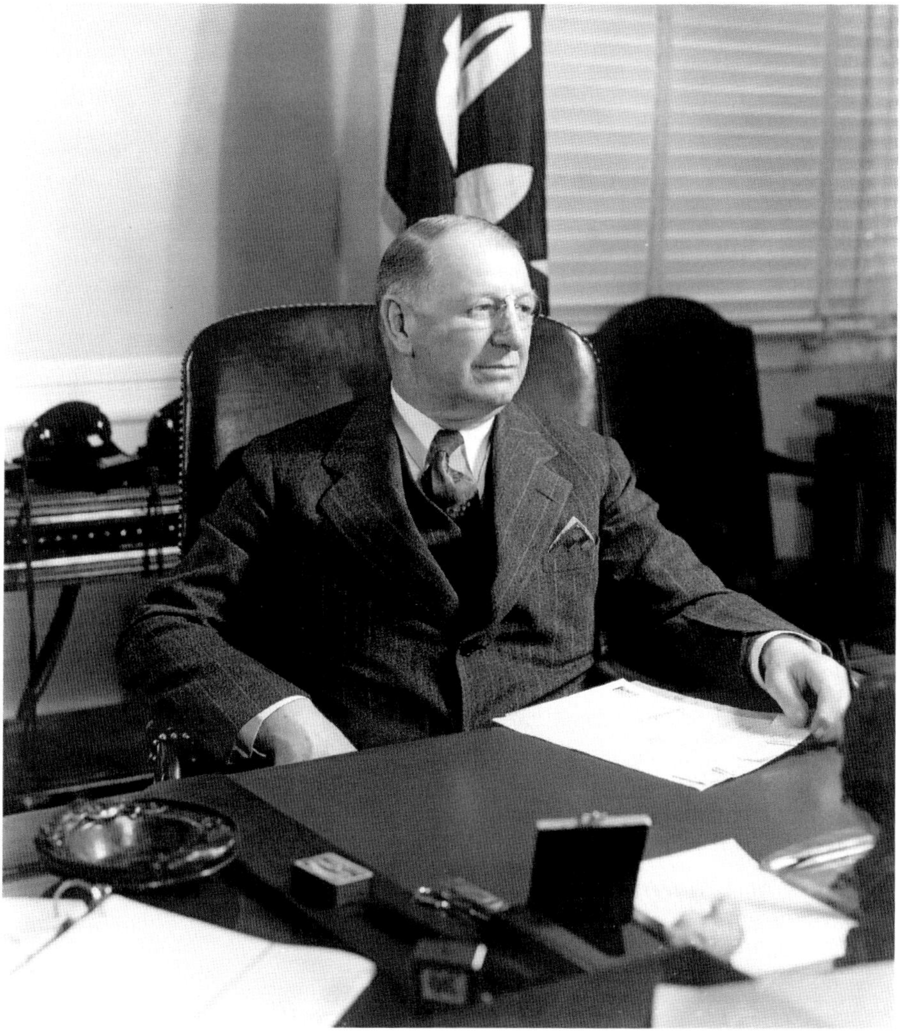

Frank Knox—a publisher, politician and patriot—began his newspaper career as a reporter for the *Grand Rapids Herald* and ended it as publisher of the *Chicago Daily News*. In 1936, he was the Republican candidate for vice president. He served his country as a member of the army in the Spanish-American War and World War I. He's pictured here at his desk as secretary of the navy during World War II. *Courtesy of Alma College Archives.*

Muehling. When the two learned that the *Lake Superior Journal* was for sale in Sault Ste. Marie, they bought the paper and moved to the Soo in 1902. There they converted the weekly paper to a daily and eventually bought out the competing *News-Record*, combining it with the *Journal* to form the *Sault Ste. Marie Evening News*. In 1912, Knox and Muehling sold the *Evening News* and established the *Manchester Leader* in New Hampshire.

Impressed by Knox's management style, William Randolph Hearst put him in charge of his three Boston newspapers in 1927 and, a year later, made him general manager of all Hearst papers: twenty-seven of them in seventeen cities. But the relationship between Knox and Hearst was stormy, and Knox resigned late in 1930.

Still co-owner of the New Hampshire paper with Muehling, Knox longed for greener and bigger pastures. When the publisher of the *Chicago Daily News* died in 1931, Knox obtained sufficient recommendations and financial backing to gain control of that paper.

In the mid-1930s, he turned his attention to politics, and in 1935, *Fortune Magazine* proclaimed him the leading candidate for the 1936 Republican nomination for president. A year later, however, the top spot on the ticket went to Kansas governor Alfred M. Landon; Knox was the vice presidential candidate.

Another former Alma College student, Claude Watson, was the Prohibition Party's VP choice that same year. But neither of the Alma alumni faired well. Popular president Franklin D. Roosevelt and Vice President Nance Garner were reelected by a wide margin.

Four years later, Knox accepted an invitation from FDR to serve as secretary of the navy. Though his previous military service had been in the army—during the Spanish-American War and World War I—he was put in charge of U.S. naval operations during World War II.

Muehling, Knox's friend and business partner for forty years, died on April 19, 1944. Knox went to Manchester for the funeral; while there, he suffered a mild heart attack without realizing it. Two days later, he was felled by a severe attack at his office in Washington, and he died two days later.

Once asked which of his talents might have led FDR to choose him as secretary of the navy, Knox replied that it may have been something he'd first learned in the *Herald* newsroom at Grand Rapids: the ability to withstand the pressure of fighting the clock.

## GR's Other Congressman Ford

It's not likely that Gerald R. Ford, who served thirteen terms in the House of Representatives before becoming vice president and then president of the United States, will ever be forgotten. However, he wasn't the first Congressman Ford from Grand Rapids, and few remember his predecessor.

Sixty years before Gerald Ford was elected to Congress, Melbourne H. Ford left his home on Lafayette Avenue to serve in the same capacity.

Both men were U.S. Navy veterans. Gerald was a lieutenant commander who saw action on the USS *Monterey* in the Pacific during World War II. At the age of sixteen, Melbourne enlisted in the navy near the end of the Civil War, and in the summer of 1865, he was aboard the USS *Colorado* when it left for a multiyear cruise of Europe. While the ship was at Naples in 1867 he learned of his appointment as a cadet to the Naval Academy. His studies at Annapolis ended after only a year because of an eye infection.

Following their military service, both also were involved in legal pursuits. After studying at the University of Michigan and Yale Law School, Gerald became an attorney. Melbourne also studied law and was admitted to the bar, but he worked as a court stenographer.

Despite the similarities of their military and civilian activities, the Fords had little in common when it came to politics. Gerald was in Congress twenty-five years as a Republican, while Melbourne served slightly more than two years as a Democrat.

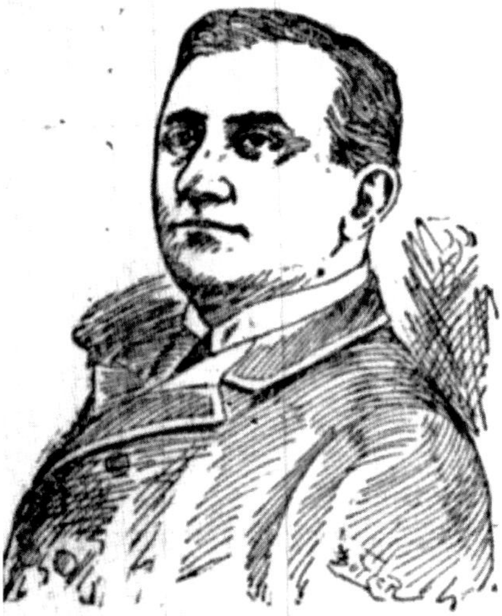

MELBOURN H. FORD.

Everyone in Grand Rapids knows about Congressman Gerald R. Ford, who later became vice president and then president of the United States—and most of the old-timers have met him. But few are aware that the city was represented by an earlier Congressman Ford. Melbourne H. Ford was a member of the House of Representatives sixty years before Gerald R. Ford went to Washington. *Courtesy of Grand Rapids History and Special Collections, Archives, Grand Rapids Public Library.*

Born in Saline on June 30, 1849, Melbourne Ford moved with his parents to Lansing in 1859. There he studied in local public schools and at Michigan Agricultural College (now Michigan State University) before enlisting in the navy. In 1873, he married Mary Carr of Newport, Rhode Island, and they settled in Grand Rapids, where he served as a stenographer in municipal, state and federal courts.

After an 1885–86 term in the Michigan legislature, Melbourne was elected to the fiftieth Congress in November 1886 by edging out Republican candidate George McBride, 18,567 votes to 18,120. When he sought reelection in 1888, Melbourne was defeated by Charles Belknap. In the November 1890 election, however, he regained his seat in the House by defeating Charles Watkins, a popular Union army officer during the Civil War.

Just seven weeks after opening of the fifty-second Congress in March 1891, Melbourne unexpectedly died in his Grand Rapids home at the age of forty-one. The April 21, 1891 edition of the *Grand Rapids Democrat* reported that he had been at home with "a slight indisposition, probably a cold," for about ten days but seemed to have recovered from that.

"Stricken by apoplexy in the night," the paper noted, "he never regained consciousness to greet his wife and bid his children good-bye, but in a comatose state he lay, until breaths becoming shorter and feebler at five minutes after twelve o'clock yesterday afternoon they ceased entirely and Melbourne H. Ford was no more." In a special election later that year, Belknap was chosen to complete Ford's term.

Tributes to Congressman Ford by colleagues in the House and Senate included one by Republican senator Francis Stockbridge, who said, "Although we were not of the same political faith, and his signal and repeated successes were disadvantageous to the political organization of my association, I shared in the general pride with which the people of Michigan observed his steady advance to national distinction."

Belknap, the Republican who defeated Ford in 1888 and returned to Washington in 1891, said that if Ford had a fault, "it was due to his generous nature, his warm heart. He studied to please men, not to displease them. He often wronged himself in an effort to satisfy those who called for his assistance."

## GR GOES TO THE BEACH

Some know it as Holland State Park; to others, it's Ottawa Beach. It's one of Michigan's most popular recreational destinations. During recent summers, it was the most preferred state park among day-use visitors and near the top among campers. But its glory days were a century ago, when vacationers came by train and Great Lakes steamboats for stays at a magnificent hotel and nearby cottages.

Through the years, Ottawa Beach has been a favored destination for Grand Rapids residents, and some of the city's leading citizens were responsible for its development. They had hoped to purchase Macatawa Park on the south side of Holland harbor channel from its developers, but their offer was rejected. So, in 1885, they founded the West Michigan Park Association, which still exists, and bought fifty-four acres on the north shore to establish a competing enterprise.

In a May 1886 meeting at the Morton House in downtown Grand Rapids, the group reviewed an architect's plan for a new hotel, which was completed on the north side of the channel by the end of June. A year later, members of the association began building cottages on lots they had purchased. When the hotel was named Ottawa, the resort area became known as Ottawa Beach. The building, often expanded and improved, became one of the most spectacular structures along Great Lakes shores.

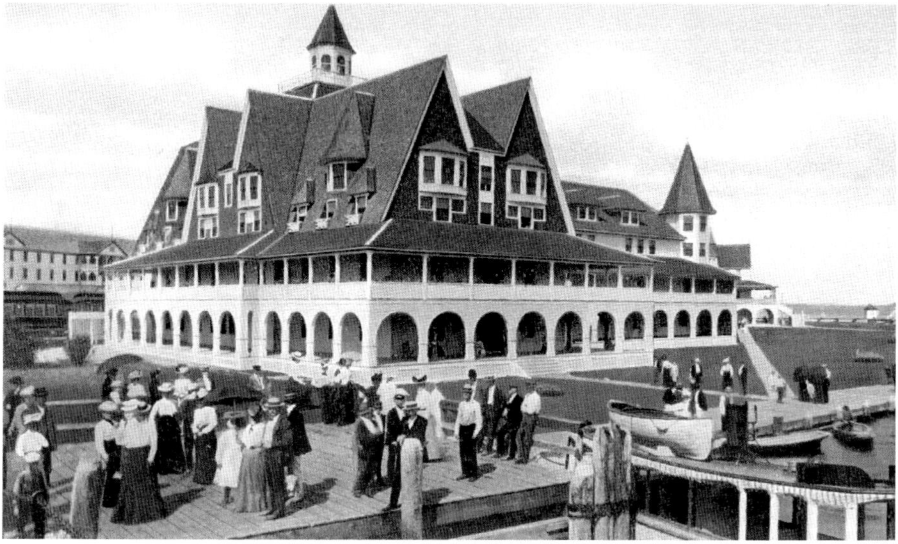

For many years, this grand hotel provided luxurious accommodations for resorters at Ottawa Beach. Constructed by Grand Rapids entrepreneurs in the 1880s, the hotel and its nearby beach attracted thousands of vacationers. But in 1923, soon after workmen renovating the building left for the day, a fire broke out and quickly reduced the splendid structure to ashes.

Among Grand Rapids leaders who played roles in the development of the resort were Chicago and West Michigan Railway executives J.B. Mulliken, J.K.V. Agnew, W.A. Gavett and Charles M. Heald; interurban railway executive Benjamin S. Hanchett; and hoteliers J. Boyd Pantlind and his son, Fred Z. Pantlind. Mulliken, Agnew and Gavett were among the founders of the West Michigan Park Association, and the others were involved in ownership changes of the hotel.

Heald purchased the hotel property in 1895 when the association was unable to make mortgage payments. The Chicago and West Michigan Railway, of which he was general manager, had extended its line from Holland to Ottawa Beach five years earlier and, immediately after the purchase, began extensive renovation of the hotel.

Soon after the Pere Marquette Railroad was formed and acquired the C&WM in 1899 it, too, improved the hotel. When the work was completed in 1901, the facility was leased to J. Boyd Pantlind.

Meanwhile, across the channel, the Grand Rapids, Holland and Chicago Interurban Line began carrying passengers to Macatawa Park at the dawn of the twentieth century. Hanchett, president of both that line and the Grand Rapids Street Railway Company, was involved in development of amusement parks—Jenison Park at Macatawa and Ramona Park in East Grand Rapids—to increase patronage.

When the Pere Marquette discontinued rail service to Ottawa Beach in 1913, Hanchett provided ferry service to the north shore from Macatawa. In June of that year, along with James Stanley Morton of the Graham and Morton Steamship Line and J. Boyd Pantlind, he purchased the hotel at Ottawa Beach.

In 1923, Fred Z. Pantlind and George F. Getz, the owner of nearby Lakewood Farm, took over operations at Ottawa Beach and began renovating the hotel. On November 6, fifteen minutes after workmen completed construction of a dance hall addition and left the building, a fire broke out and quickly engulfed the entire structure. It was never rebuilt.

Pantlind, who was a member of the State Park Board, suggested that the state buy the beach property and develop it as a park. He donated a bathhouse at the beach, and the state invested $830,000 for improvements before the opening of Holland State Park in 1928.

Best known of the Grand Rapids–area residents who enjoyed Ottawa Beach was President Gerald R. Ford, who vacationed there many summers from the 1930s to the mid-1960s, first at the cottage of his parents and later at one he co-owned with his brothers.

## Risks of Catching Rays

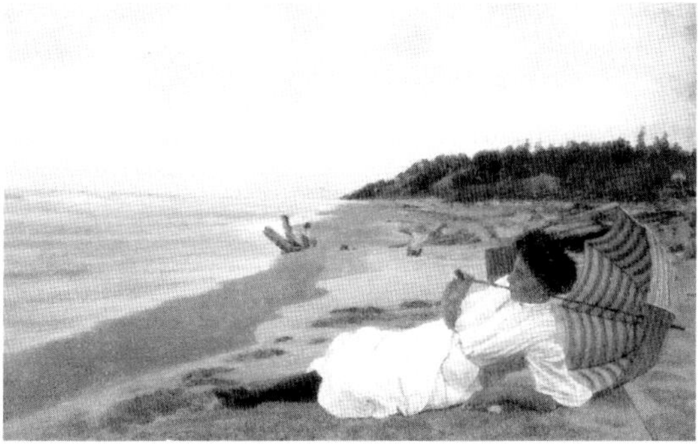

Sunbathing at Ottawa Beach through the first few decades of the twentieth century didn't permit tanning of much more than faces and hands. People at the beach for relaxation rather than swimming often wore their Sunday

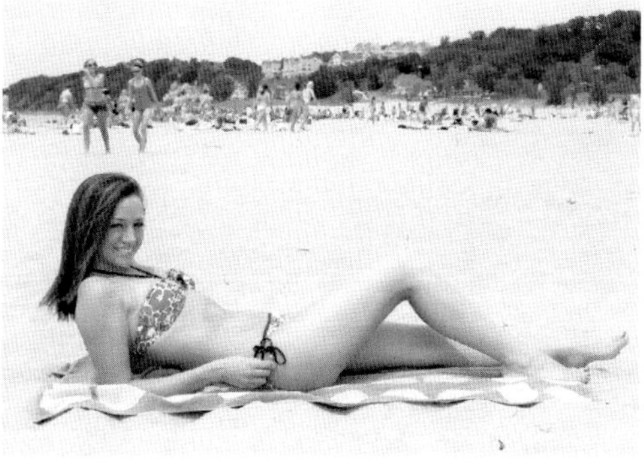

best. Men might be attired in white shirts, ties and suits. Hems of women's skirts often reached their ankles.

Before the 1940s, if anyone would have worn swimwear comparable to today's, they'd have been thrown out of Holland State Park. Park Superintendent Neal Sybesma warned in 1932 that male bathers needed to wear more than trunks and that the straps of their bathing suits could not dangle over their shoulders. They couldn't remain in the park, he said, in that "semi-nude state." Women were expected to be even more covered than the men.

There are no rules regarding swimwear at state parks today, and most park users feel that this has improved aesthetics at the beach.

*Top*: Less than a century ago, sunbathers at Ottawa Beach could tan little more than faces and forearms.

*Bottom*: Fashions at the beach, though, have changed through the years. *Author's collection.*

## The Wizard and Tamawaca

Macatawa Park, nestled between Lake Michigan and Lake Macatawa on the south shore of Holland harbor's channel, is a tranquil resort with limited access. But at the dawn of the twentieth century, throngs seeking excitement and relaxation came from Grand Rapids and Chicago.

Among those enticed from the Windy City to Lake Michigan's eastern shore was L. Frank Baum, author of the Oz series, which included *The Wonderful Wizard of Oz*. He learned about Macatawa from friends and visited the resort in 1899. During the next two summers, he rented a cottage there and, in 1902, bought one overlooking Lake Michigan.

Royalties from *Father Goose: His Book*, his 1899 best-selling children's volume, provided most of the funds for the cottage, so he named it the Sign of the Goose and used geese liberally in its decor. Dorothy Hall, granddaughter of the owners of the cottage next to Baum's, often sat in a goose-shaped rocking chair and listened as he recited stories. Many at Macatawa believed that she inspired the lead character in his best-known book and subsequent film, *The Wizard of Oz*, starring Judy Garland.

Most of the sixty-two books written by Baum were children's stories, but one—written under the pen name John Estes Cooke—focused on Macatawa, disguising the resort by calling it Tamawaca. In the story, Macatawa Bay became Iroquois Bay, and the city of Holland was called Kochton. Resorts farther from the setting—such as Bay View, Charlevoix and Petoskey—kept their actual names.

In an introductory section of *Tamawaca Folks: A Summer Comedy*, Baum disclaimed any connection between the tale's characters and real people, but many resorters identified Macatawa residents.

"Tamawaca exists and is as beautiful as I have described it," Baum said in the introduction. But in the story he levels barbs at individuals whose actions and attitudes obviously offended him. One, named Wilder, is described as "the pirate of Tamawaca," a man who owns a third of the resort. His confederate, Easton, owns two-thirds and is a "fine old religious duffer who loves to pray for your spiritual welfare while he feels for your pocketbook."

Baum also derided a group of girls attracted to a handsome young man, Jim, until they learn that he's only a clerk at Marshall Field's in Chicago. When Jim's parents visit Tamawaca after he has developed a relationship with a less snobby young lady, his father objects—until he discovers the girl is a daughter of "the richest Standard Oil magnate after Rockefeller himself."

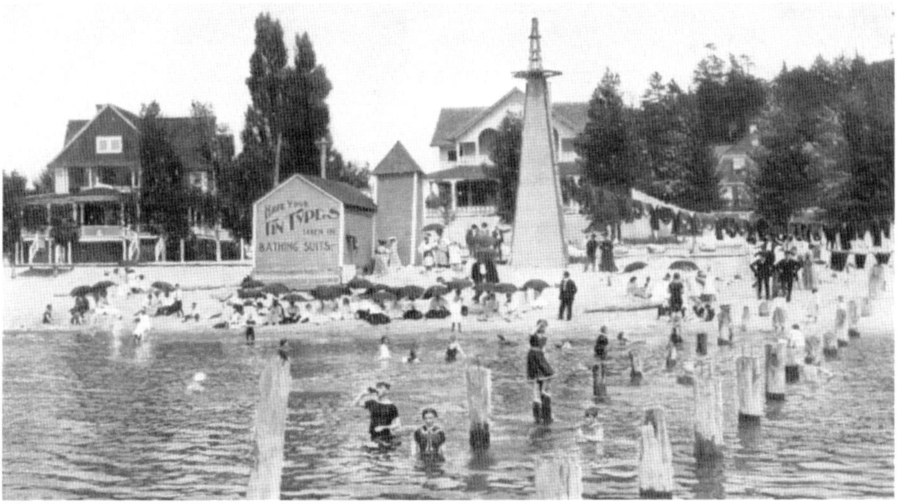


Lakes Michigan and Macatawa attracted thousands to Macatawa Park, among them L. Frank Baum, who purchased a cottage there with proceeds from the sale of his best-selling *Father Goose: His Book*. Many of Baum's Macatawa friends believed that Dorothy Hall, the granddaughter of his next-door neighbor at Macatawa, was the inspiration for his lead character in *The Wonderful Wizard of Oz*.

In a poem written for the *Grand Rapids Herald* in 1907, Baum treated Macatawa and its folks more gently:

*A summer haven that's designed*
*So perfectly to charm mankind…*
*Where all is love and peace and joy*
*Without a "skeeter" to annoy*
*Or sign of any carking care*
*To be discovered anywhere.*

Hundreds of children who read Baum's books sent him letters, and he answered each one. He explained to an interviewer that if, when he was a child, he had received a letter from an author whose book he had read, he would have been thrilled. Making children happy, he added, was his greatest desire.

After the summer of 1907, Baum moved to California, and ownership of his Macatawa cottage changed several times before it and thirty-four others were destroyed in a 1927 fire.

## Newsman to Newsmaker

Billing clerk Arthur H. Vandenberg left his job early on September 7, 1900, in order to greet vice presidential candidate Theodore Roosevelt's campaign train that was steaming into Grand Rapids. Then, when Vandenberg returned to the Sears Bakery of the National Biscuit Company, he faced an angry boss—and was soon unemployed.

What he did next propelled him into the world of journalism and eventually into national politics, where, as a senator after World War II, he helped gain approval of the Marshall Plan and the North Atlantic Treaty Organization and also was a key player in the formation of the United Nations. He still is the most revered politician from Michigan next to the late president Gerald R. Ford, who often cited Vandenberg as a role model and mentor.

As a young man, Vandenberg hoped to study law at the University of Michigan. But he needed more funds for tuition, so he went to the *Grand Rapids Herald* and asked for a job. He was hired as a writer and worked there briefly. After completing study at U of M, Vandenberg worked for *Collier's* magazine. He returned to the *Herald* in 1904 and, two years later, became head of the editorial staff, serving until 1928.

Fascinated by politics ever since the 1900 Roosevelt rally, Vandenberg began maneuvering for a Senate seat in the late 1920s. When the incumbent senator died eight months before the election, Vandenberg expected Governor Fred W. Green to appoint him to the position—as Green had promised during the 1926 race for governor. But Green decided to appoint Congressman Joe Fordney instead, on the condition that Fordney would not seek election, leaving Vandenberg to battle it out with other prospects.

Shortly thereafter, Vandenberg received an envelope from the governor, but in disgust, he threw it unopened into his wastebasket. Then a Detroit newspaper reported that Green had decided at the last minute to appoint Vandenberg! *Herald* staff members helped their boss frantically search through bales of wastepaper. When the envelope was found, Vandenberg tore it open and learned he would indeed become a senator. He was elected that fall and reelected in 1934, 1940 and 1946, serving a total of twenty-eight years.

An outspoken isolationist before World War II, Vandenberg's views changed during and after the war, and he became one of the principal proponents of the bipartisan foreign policy that led to NATO and the United Nations.

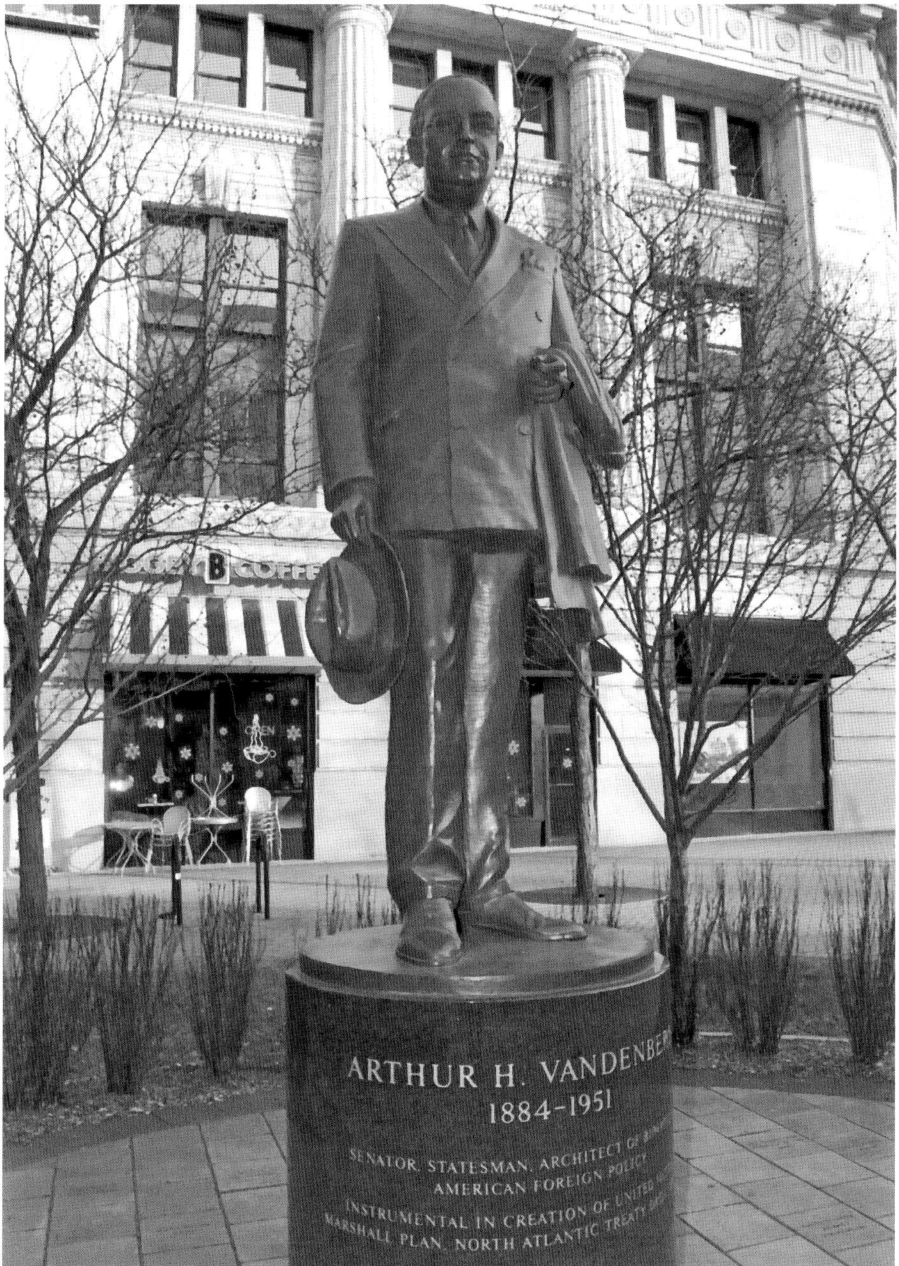


This nine-foot-tall statue of Senator Arthur Vandenberg, which was unveiled in May 2005, stands near the entrance to McKay Tower at Campau Square. Editor of the *Grand Rapids Herald* before his service in the Senate, Vandenberg was an isolationist who changed his views during World War II and became an advocate of NATO and the United Nations. *Author's collection.*

Midway through his last term, Vandenberg fell ill and had to restrict his Congressional duties. He died at his Grand Rapids home on April 18, 1951.

The *Grand Rapids Herald* ceased publishing in 1959. But Vandenberg's work as a journalist is a key reason why the *Herald* survives in the memories of those who once read its reports every morning.

## WHEN THE ROOSEVELT WOMEN VISITED

Though the appearance of presidents (and those who wanted to be) brought great excitement to Grand Rapids, just as much enthusiasm was generated by the visits of two Roosevelt women—Theodore Roosevelt's daughter and Franklin Delano Roosevelt's wife.

Alice Roosevelt Longworth, daughter of President Teddy Roosevelt, was in the city on February 12, 1909—her twenty-fifth birthday—to lay the cornerstone for the new Federal Building and attend the city's annual Lincoln Day banquet. Eleanor Roosevelt, wife of President Franklin D. Roosevelt, came for a March 9, 1936 speech at Fountain Street Baptist Church.

Alice was seventeen when the Theodore Roosevelt family moved to the White House in 1901. She hardly fit the mold for young ladies of her time, and her failure to conform to expected protocol may have contributed to her popularity among many of her gender. After being interrupted several times by his daughter during a conference with a guest, the president once commented, "I can either run the country or I can attend to Alice, but I cannot possibly do both."

When Alice was ordered to stop smoking in the White House, she went to the roof of the building and continued puffing. Since she enjoyed shocking others, Alice was no more restrained in public. She smoked at a time when ladies didn't, shot a gun from a train at insulators on telegraph poles, bragged about speeding in a friend's roadster, was known to go to parties carrying a snake, placed bets with a bookie and incurred debts playing poker and overspending on clothes. Later in life, she was pictured in magazine tobacco advertisements.

One of her cherished possessions was a pillow with the slogan "If you can't say something good about someone, sit right here by me."

Since her antics often provided reporters with good copy, they loved her and sometimes referred to her as "Princess Alice" or "the Other Washington Monument." When she returned from a trip to Asia with bundles of silk for dresses, they called her "Alice in Plunder Land."

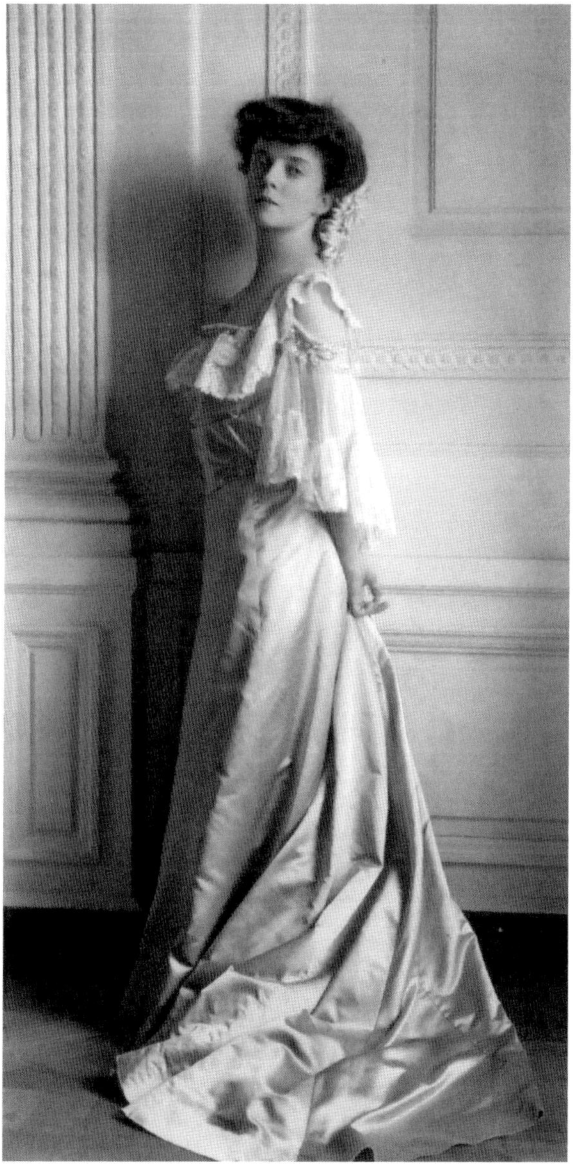

Teddy Roosevelt's exuberant daughter, Alice, was a crowd favorite when she came to Grand Rapids in 1909. However, she was a frequent frustration for her father. On one occasion, when she kept interrupting him during a conference with a guest, the president noted he could either run the country or manage Alice but not both. *Courtesy of Library of Congress.*

Her fondness for a particular shade of blue inspired the 1919 hit song "Alice Blue Gown," written for the Broadway musical *Irene*. When the Roosevelts left Washington, Alice entombed a voodoo doll of Nellie Taft, the incoming first lady, in the White House lawn. Alice married Nicholas Longworth, an Ohio congressman with a playboy reputation who was involved in numerous affairs after the ceremony. Alice was similarly accused.

But she was a big hit when she came to Grand Rapids. "Alice Roosevelt Longworth, famous daughter of a famous sire, has come, has seen, and has conquered," reported the *Grand Rapids Herald*. "Before her participation in the Federal Building cornerstone laying and the Lincoln Banquet, she and her husband were taken on a trolley tour of the city and visited Mrs. H.C. Dykhouse's Romeo Cattery…She looked every inch the typical American girl, full of health, vivacity and spirits, and was good to look upon. It was a great day for the cats, and they seemed to enjoy it as much as did the visitors."

Alice's relationships with both her stepmother and her mother-in-law were strained. Her biological mother and her Grandmother Roosevelt both died two days after her birth. When Alice married, her stepmother said, "I want you to know I am glad to see you leave. You have never been anything but trouble." Alice's nickname for her mother-in-law was "Bromide."

When Eleanor Roosevelt came in 1936 to speak at Fountain Street Baptist Church, she visited the Works Progress Administration's whooping cough immunization project at West Michigan Laboratories on Fuller Avenue, the City Highway Garage (another WPA project) and the Better Housing Show at the Civic Auditorium.

Paul De Kruif, Zeeland native and author of *Microbe Hunters*, was at the Fuller Avenue laboratories when Mrs. Roosevelt arrived. Urging her to do what she could to increase funding for the immunization project, he said that it would popularize the WPA and "answer the objections made to boondoggling."

The president's wife countered that opposition to the WPA didn't come from ordinary citizens. "There may be one here and there," she said, "who sees a man leaning on his shovel and says, 'I work harder than that.' But most of the opposition to WPA comes from those who are unwilling to pay the taxes to maintain it."

## What a Wingding!

Grand Rapids is certainly a celebrating city, with lots of grand events that attract not only area residents but also thousands from afar. Among these events is each year's Grand Rapids Festival, which brings hundreds of artists and performers to stages and display areas and offers a variety of ethnic food treats at the heart of the city in June. Then, of course, there's autumn's ArtPrize, which lures thousands of visitors and which recently attracted more than 1,500 exhibitors from forty-two states and thirty-six countries in competition for the world's largest monetary award. And these are but two of the city's many special events.

Festivities of this kind have thrilled thousands in Grand Rapids for years, the first really big bash taking place in 1876 when the city celebrated the national centennial as well as the 50$^{th}$ anniversary of the arrival of its first permanent settler, Louis Campau. The 1926 observance of the 100$^{th}$ anniversary of Campau's coming was another memorable event.

Between those two observances was yet another grand affair, the Grand Rapids Homecoming and Sixtieth Anniversary Celebration, which was held in August 1910. Actually, it was sort of an afterthought. Civic leaders had hoped to observe the fiftieth anniversary of the city's charter in 1900, but plans never developed beyond the dreaming stage and the year passed without anything happening.

To make up for that lost opportunity for a big party, a group of local leaders made preparations for the 1910 event. Chairman of the planning committee was Benjamin S. Hanchett, president and general manager of Grand Rapids Street Railway Company. Among those working with him were William Alden Smith, U.S. senator and owner of the *Grand Rapids Herald*; Arthur H. Vandenberg, *Herald* editor and later a U.S. senator; and Edmond W. Booth, editor of the *Grand Rapids Press*.

Promotional efforts included the production of a series of colorful postcards that could be mailed to former residents as an invitation to return for the event. Several of the cards featured recently constructed buildings and two characters—Progress, an attractive lady, and Labor, a man whose physique and attire bore a striking resemblance to Tarzan of the Apes, a popular twentieth-century film and comic strip character yet to be created. He first appeared in a novel published by *All-Story Magazine* in 1912, then in silent films during 1918 and finally in a comic strip early in 1929.

During the celebration, the façades of most downtown buildings were draped with decorative bunting in red, white, and blue, as well as the special Homecoming colors of green, pink and white. About 3,500 out-of-towners came back to Grand Rapids for the weeklong reunion, which began a minute after midnight on Monday, August 23, with a concert by the Press Newsboys Band on the lawn of the Fisk Lake home of the Hanchett family. The musicians then boarded streetcars and filled the air with music throughout the city, awakening residents within earshot.

Sleepers were roused the next night, too, when a violent storm moved in. "Precluded by vivid electrical flashes and accompanied by thunderous

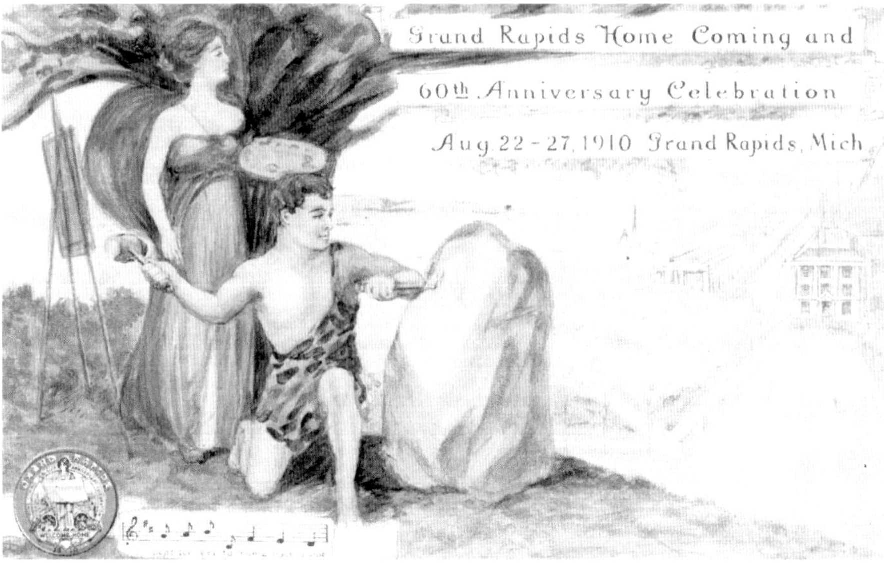


Pictured on some of the postcards produced to persuade former residents to return for a 1910 Grand Rapids homecoming were Progress, a lady, and Labor, a man who resembled a yet-to-be-created Tarzan of the Apes. The popular character didn't appear in a comic strip until 1929.

reverberations as befits a festival rain," the *Grand Rapids Herald* reported, "it fell refreshingly on the just and the few unjust foregathered in the Homecoming city."

The following night featured a noisy welcome for visitors as factory whistles blew, church bells rang, bands played and children crowded the streets with what the *Herald* called "horns, squawkers, and every sort of noise producer." Adding to the thrill was a red glow in the sky. At the outskirts of the city, thirty-nine light towers had been erected. "At a preset time," the newspaper noted, "the elevators were sent aloft with their burdens of powder, to which had been set a time fuse. The effect was startling."

Many activities of the week focused on themes for each day. Monday was Reunion Day; Tuesday, Old Settlers Day; Wednesday, Civic Day; Thursday, Fraternal and Grand Rapids Day; and Friday, Historical and Allegorical Day. There were balloon ascensions, which included parachute drops in the daytime and searchlight effects at night. Other features of the week were band concerts, open-air high-wire acts and parades.

The week's four processions attracted throngs. Though the city had a population of only 112,600 in 1910, Wednesday's three-mile-long daytime Civic Parade attracted an estimated 75,000 persons and even more for what the *Herald* called an "evening repetition." Thursday's Fraternal and Military Parade and Floral Pageant drew a crowd of about 125,000.

During Wednesday night's parade and celebrations at Campau Square, the city's police ambulance was called out several times. The *Herald* noted that it "came clanging down Pearl Street past the end of the big grandstand and the box at the Old National Bank, where persons either ill or naughty were quickly taken to the hospital or police station, as their case demanded."

## Christmas a Century Ago

Christmas in Grand Rapids one hundred years ago was dazzling white!

Shortly after noon on December 25, 1910, snow started falling in earnest, and the storm ended up as "a real gee-whizzer," according to the *Grand Rapids Herald* the next morning. Wind from the southeast at eight miles per hour increased to twenty and whipped the snow into drifts. Most trains were late, the *Herald* noted, some of them by forty-five minutes.

Before the storm, downtown stores were open evenings before Christmas, but there were comparatively few last-minute shoppers. "I really expected to see more people down," one merchant said. "The weather was just right for a big turnout, but it failed to materialize."

Prices were right, though, according to December 24 newspaper ads. At Smith's Department Store, women's sweaters, regularly $4.00, were going for $2.69. Steketee's offered ladies' silk vests for $1.50 and men's Elgin shirts for $0.85. Herpolsheimer's was selling toy trains with an engine, coal tender and four cars for $1.25 and dolls for between $0.25 and $0.29.

In Washington, President William Howard Taft finished his Christmas shopping on December 23. Fond of giving books and jewelry as gifts, he spent much of his time rummaging the shelves of booksellers and jewelers, according to news reports. One also noted that, like many other shoppers, he started on his tour of shops with a long list of names and probable purchases.

Special musical programs at midtown Grand Rapids churches attracted several of the 112,600 residents of the city on Christmas morning. A new organ at St. Mark's Cathedral was used for the first time at the service there, with Phelps Cowan at the organ and yule songs sung by a choir of forty-five men and boys. Music at Fountain Street Baptist Church was led by Mrs. William Fenton, who took over as director of music for the congregation that day. At St. Andrews Cathedral, organist Paul C. Flerle played Christmas selections on the chimes, beginning at 4:30 a.m.

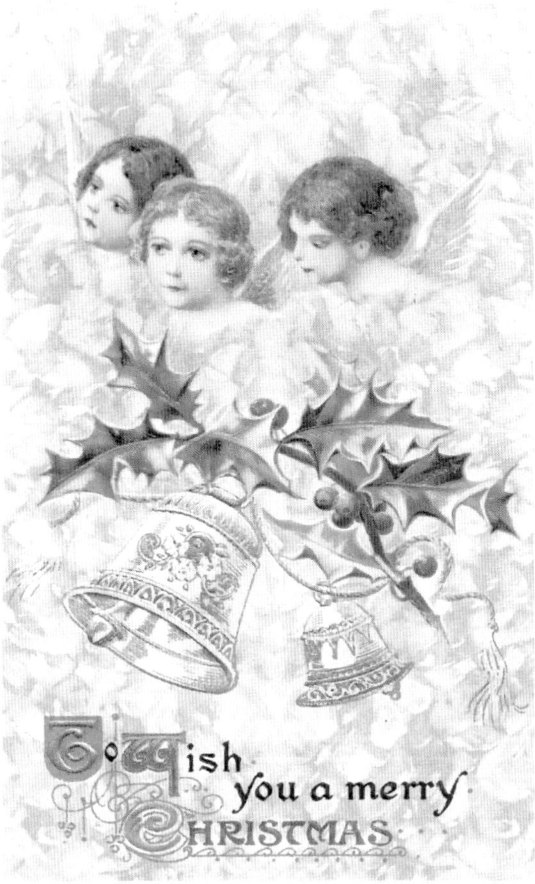


Typical of the postcard-format Christmas greetings mailed in 1910 is this one picturing angelic young ladies, a holly branch and bells. In Grand Rapids that year, contributors to the *Herald* Santa Claus Girls campaign brought joy to six hundred children.

Residents of Grand Rapids were generous as they remembered underprivileged neighbors in 1910. "The *Herald* Santa Claus Girls found no 'scrooges,'" the newspaper reported in its Christmas morning edition, adding that contributions gave six hundred children a happy Christmas.

A day earlier, the *Herald* had reported that more than two hundred children "were stirred and made to glow with happiness" when the local corps of the Salvation Army held its annual yule celebration for Sunday school students and any others who cared to attend.

On the day after Christmas, not all citizens were happy, however. Attorney Howard A. Thornton, who lived on South College Avenue, had left the city with his family the day before Christmas to spend the holiday with his parents. When they returned, they discovered that burglars had broken into their home early Christmas morning, ransacked it and took virtually everything of value.

But there was one happy ending to the holiday. Arriving in the city on Christmas Eve on a train from Saginaw was eleven-year-old Albert Galzan, an orphan who was to be adopted by a family in Conklin. However, the man who was to meet him at Union Depot failed to show up. Alone, with no money and unacquainted with anyone in the city, Albert was befriended by station master C.C. Pratt, who bought supper for the boy and put him to bed in his office.

With the help of police and the staff of St. John's Orphan Home, the boy was soon placed on an interurban car of the Grand Rapids, Grand Haven and Muskegon Railway and taken to his new home at Conklin the next day.

## Steaming Over the Lakes

Where is Grand Rapids? The answer during the twentieth century might have been: "Probably in the middle of Lake Michigan."

During that period, three steamships named SS *City of Grand Rapids* cruised the lakes. Most popular was the luxurious flagship of the Graham and Morton Steamship Line known as the "Honeymoon Ship."

Operating between Chicago and St. Joseph, the company offered package deals to couples planning quickie marriages. Since waiting time between license application and wedding ceremony was shorter in Michigan than in Illinois, many took advantage of the service. From the dock at St. Joseph, couples were taken to a clergyman or justice of the peace. Then they returned to Chicago in a bridal suite aboard the *Grand Rapids*.

Advertised as the largest excursion ship on Lake Michigan, its accommodations were so elaborate that it also was known as the "First Lady of the Great Lakes." Launched in 1912, it provided overnight service from Chicago to Holland, where railroads offered connections to the city of Grand Rapids.

When Graham and Morton merged with Goodrich Transit Company in 1925, the ship was shifted to a Chicago–Muskegon–Grand Haven route. Goodrich went out of business in the early 1930s, and ownership of the *Grand Rapids* changed hands several times in subsequent years. It cruised the western shore of Lake Michigan for the Chicago-Milwaukee Steamship Line until 1942.

The first SS *Grand Rapids* to cruise the lakes was built in 1879 at Grand Haven for Hannah, Lay and Company of Traverse City. After running between Traverse City and Mackinac Island for fourteen years, it was sold to

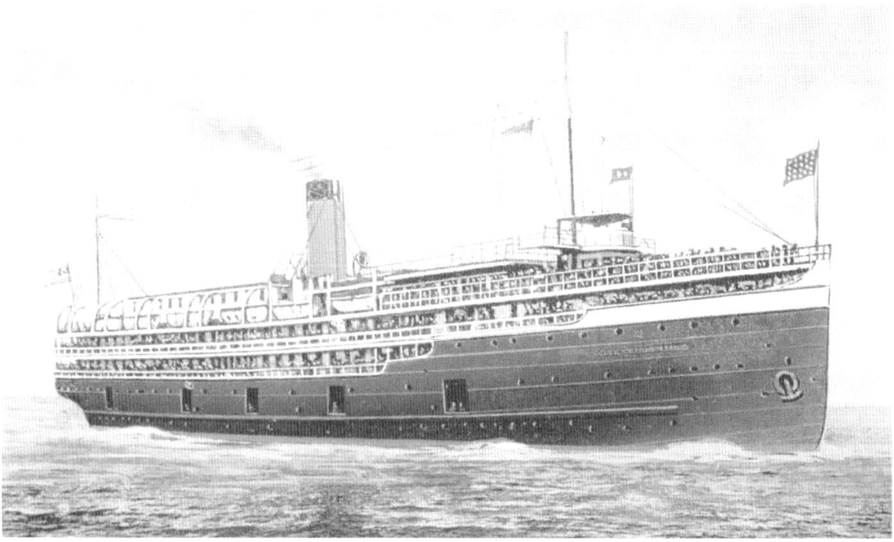

Best known of the three Great Lakes ships named *City of Grand Rapids* was this one, which was called the "Honeymoon Ship" after its launching in 1912. Chicago couples often took advantage of special quickie marriage deals and sailed to Michigan, where the waiting time between marriage applications and ceremonies was shorter.

Oscar Wilbur and operated between Charlevoix and Marquette. In 1897, it was purchased by the South Haven and Chicago Transportation Company for service between those two cities.

Rebuilt in 1899 to operate between South Haven and Milwaukee, its first voyage on that route ended prematurely when it began to leak; it nearly sank before returning to the Michigan port. Sold several times between 1903 and 1907, the *Grand Rapids* operated on Lake Erie during those years before shifting to Georgian Bay, where, during an overnight stop at Tobermory in October 1907, it was set afire by vandals and destroyed.

The third SS *Grand Rapids* was a car ferry built at Manitowoc, Wisconsin, in 1926 to transport railroad cars across Lake Michigan. The first of its two collisions on the lake was with its Grand Trunk Milwaukee Car Ferry sister ship, the SS *Madison*. Approaching Grand Haven through icy waters in January 1930, the *Grand Rapids* struck the *Madison*'s stern. Then, in July 1959 the *Grand Rapids* collided with the steamer *Dow Chemical*.

During its years on Lake Michigan, the *Grand Rapids* car ferry twice hit bars offshore at Grand Haven and then rammed the pier, causing damage of $11,000 the first time and $49,200 the second. It also ran aground near the harbor at Milwaukee and twice became stuck in Lake Michigan ice.

In 1967, it was cut in half at Manitowoc so the spar deck could be raised to accommodate higher cars. Three years later Grand Trunk took it out of service, intending to use its parts as spares for other ships. It was damaged by fires in 1980 and 1987, and in September 1989 it was towed out of Muskegon to be scrapped.

## Moving Up the Hard Way

It was in mid-September 1916 when a fly crept over the bricks of two tall Monroe Avenue buildings, quickly moving from the pavement to the tops of flagpoles on the roofs. This, however, was no ordinary insect. Actually, it was Harry H. Gardiner, who called himself the "Human Fly," and his feat attracted thousands to downtown Grand Rapids.

Sponsored by the *Grand Rapids Press*, he scaled the ten-story Herpolsheimer Building at noon on Monday, September 18, and the twelve-story Grand Rapids Savings Bank during Wednesday evening. An estimated twenty thousand persons saw the Monday event, and between thirty and forty thousand jammed the avenue and side streets on Wednesday.

During the following week, Gardiner climbed the walls and dome of the capitol in Lansing as thirty thousand watched, and in October, the *Detroit News* sponsored the Human Fly's noontime ascent of the Majestic Building on Woodward Avenue. A throng of about 150,000 saw him reach the top in thirty-seven minutes. He had begun climbing buildings in 1905, and during the same decade as his Michigan appearances he ascended the twenty-two-story Flatiron Building in Manhattan.

On Halloween 1918 in Vancouver, British Columbia, he attracted more people to the center of the city than had ever been there before. They watched him scale the seventeen-story World Building, now known as the Sun Tower.

On Armistice Day, a week and a half later, Gardiner celebrated the Allied victory in World War I by climbing the Bank of Hamilton Building in Ontario. Partway up the structure, he reached into an open window and signed insurance papers. Because of his risky pastime, he had been unable to get insurance elsewhere.

In a 1925 fundraising venture for the American Legion at Enid, Oklahoma, Gardiner scaled the Enid Bank and Trust Company building while legionnaires passed through the crowd with containers for contributions. The Human Fly paused occasionally in his ascent to call out and urge those below to give more money. On the other side of the town square, Paul Whiteman and his orchestra were presenting a concert in the city's Convention Hall. That, too, was a fundraiser.

In Grand Rapids, Gardiner climbed the Herpolsheimer Building in nineteen minutes and the bank building in twenty minutes. "All that saved the climber from a fall into the crowd below," the *Press* reported after the Herpolsheimer ascent, "was a grip of a hand on the smallest extension or a perilous foothold on almost smooth masonry. On the seventh floor he swung back and forth in the ozone over the heads of a gasping crowd a full one hundred feet below. On the sixth, flat against the brick, he released his hold on the terra cotta molding and stood with the tips of his toes on a ledge no wider than a dollar."

A searchlight atop the Herpolsheimer Building focused on Gardiner as he climbed the taller structure Wednesday night. "Within twenty minutes," the *Press* reported, "he swung on the wide roof cornice, stretched his hard-worked muscles a moment and scampered to the lofty flagstaff. He swarmed up this like a monkey."

The crowd below was said by the newspaper to be the largest that had ever assembled in Grand Rapids. It filled the main street from Division

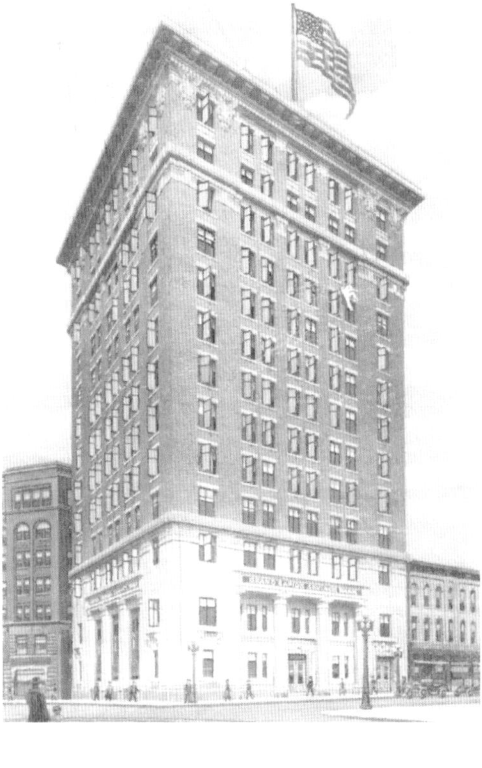

This postcard, which purports to show "Human Fly" Harry Gardiner climbing the Grand Rapids Savings Bank building at Campau Square, was probably produced before the event and sold to interested persons in the crowd. It can't be a photo taken at the time of the climb: more than thirty thousand crowded the streets at the time, but only a few are in the picture.

Avenue to Campau Square and overflowed into side streets, onto roofs of buildings and in windows within sight of the bank building.

During his always-upward career, Gardiner scaled more than seven hundred buildings in North America and Europe.

## Grand Rapids Up in the Air

When the Wright brothers brought a biplane to the West Michigan Fair at Comstock Park on September 3, 1911, hundreds of Grand Rapids residents dropped everything and headed to the fairgrounds.

Aviation was still in its infancy then, and seeing a plane in the sky was as awesome as spotting a UFO might be today. This time, there would be a chance to see the famous Wrights…and perhaps even go up in an aircraft.

Many area residents may find it surprising that Grand Rapids has a strong connection to the history of aviation, both with pioneering aviators and in the development of airlines.

Best known among the local aviators was Bert "Fish" Hassell. He picked up the moniker when he crashed a seaplane into Lake Michigan north of Chicago in 1915. A year later, Grand Rapids businessmen Fred Pantlind and Jewell Clark invited Hassell to help rebuild a flying boat on the shore of Reeds Lake and then pilot it.

Hassell later trained pilots for action in World War I. He returned to Grand Rapids in 1919 as chief pilot of Roseswift Airplane Company, flying freight and passengers to and from Ionia; he also offered weekend plane rides at nearby small towns. The company went out of business a year later, but Hassell and another Roseswift pilot thrilled crowds at Ramona Amusement Park's season-opening day in May 1920 with a mock aerial battle over Reeds Lake.

Involved with airplanes throughout his life, Hassell for a time was a barnstormer and then a bootlegger, flying booze in from Canada and the Atlantic Ocean. A year after Charles Lindbergh crossed the Atlantic, Hassell attempted to fly from his hometown of Rockford, Illinois, to Sweden in an effort to demonstrate the advantages of a northern route between the two continents—the route used for most commercial flights today. But he was forced down in Greenland and spent two weeks on the ice cap before being rescued.

He served in the air force during both World War II and the Korean conflict and then was involved in construction of the Distant Early Warning (DEW) Line.

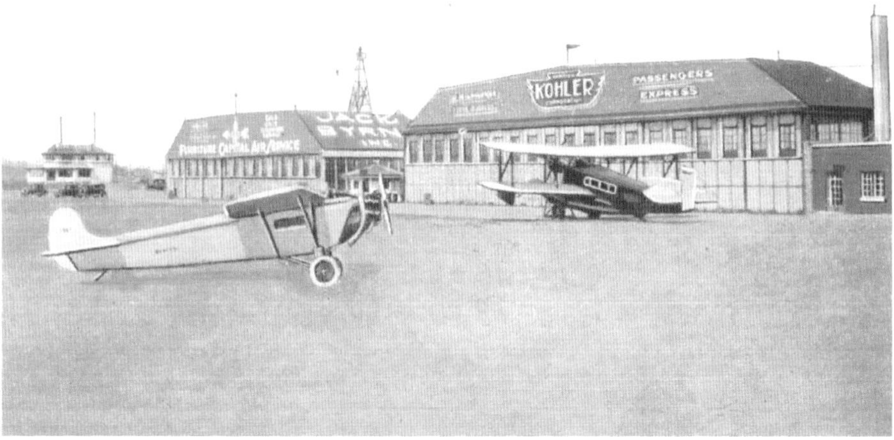


Parked in front of the Kohler Aviation hangar at the old Kent County Airport is a Keystone-Loening amphibian that carried passengers between Grand Rapids and Milwaukee during the 1920s and '30s. The cabin above a large pontoon accommodated six passengers, but the pilot and copilot sat outside in an exposed cockpit.

Among other early Grand Rapids pilots were teenagers Clara Kutschinski and Lawrence Maile. Kutschinski was a seventeen-year-old Central High School student when she passed the exam for a license to become the youngest female pilot in the state and the first in Grand Rapids. Maile was a nineteen-year-old newsboy in charge of east-end circulation for the *Grand Rapids Herald* when he took flying lessons at Furniture Capital Air Service.

A 1929 *Herald* story reported about an innovative tool used in Maile's instruction: a helmet described as "a telephonic headgear." The trainee, who sat in the front cockpit, wore the helmet with receivers in each side. Instructor Floyd Becker, in the cockpit behind, spoke into a mouthpiece, and an electric cord embedded in a long tube connected the two. When the instructor gave directions, according to the story, he "idled the motor to reduce the roar, then spoke his directions for operation of the ship into the mouthpiece."

The involvement of Grand Rapids in the development of airlines included the first regularly scheduled U.S. line—Stout Air Services—which flew between Grand Rapids and Detroit in the mid-1920s. Its planes, designed and built by William Stout, were the first commercially successful all-metal aircraft. Most earlier planes had been made of wood and canvas.

At the end of the 1920s, Kohler Aviation Corporation was carrying Grand Rapids–Milwaukee passengers across Lake Michigan in Keystone-Loening amphibians—popularly called "ducks" (looking a bit like them). The planes, with pilot and copilot in exterior cockpits, had an enclosed cabin for six passengers.

In the early 1930s, the ducks were replaced by larger birds. Next to appear in the skies over Grand Rapids were trimotor planes, produced by Ford Motor Company in cooperation with Stout. This plane was widely known as the "Tin Goose" or "Flying Washboard." Like the earliest planes that flew over the city, it elicited stares into the sky.

## A Plant That Bombed

Buried beneath one of Kent County's popular recreation areas and an adjacent golf course are tons of jagged concrete that would have become a huge explosives plant had its construction not been halted at the cessation of World War I hostilities.

In 1918, construction of a multistructure facility began on a 1,380-acre site that is now Palmer Park and the Leonard E. Kaufmann Golf Course. The Kent County plant—and similar facilities being built near Little Rock, Arkansas, and Brunswick, Georgia—were intended to replace production of picric acid at a huge French plant that had been leveled by an explosion and fire.

Picric acid was used extensively in the manufacture of bombs and grenades during the war. The Michigan complex, between Forty-fourth and Fifty-second Streets just west of Clyde Park Avenue, was designed to produce 5 million pounds of picric acid per month. Area residents were enthusiastic about the project, and some, including women, worked alongside construction crews.

When the conflict ended on November 11, 1918, about 1,500 construction workers set aside their tools and walked seven miles from the plant site to downtown Grand Rapids for a victory celebration. They never went back to work.

Uncompleted foundations, pillars and walls remained at the site for nearly half a century, attracting nostalgic old-timers, curiosity seekers and sometimes mischievous children—as well as firearm enthusiasts, who used the concrete walls as backstops for their targets.

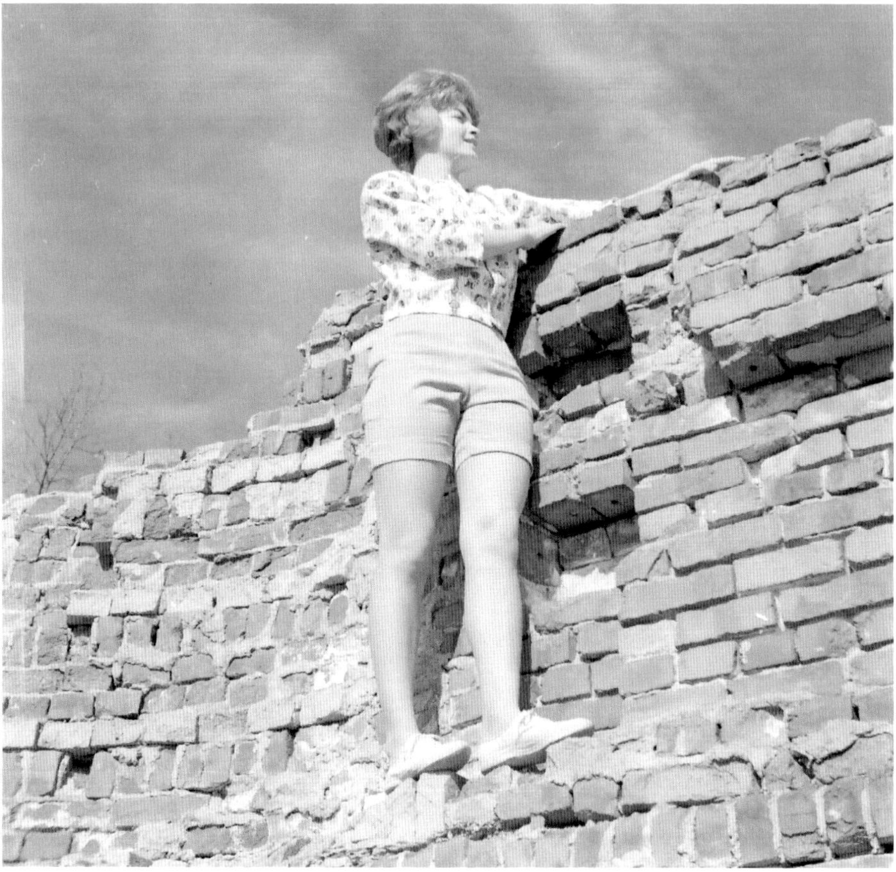

Ruins of a never-completed industrial complex in the southwest Grand Rapids suburbs are surveyed by a visitor to the site during the 1950s, a few years before the ruins were buried. Construction of the plant, which was to have produced picric acid for the manufacture of explosives, halted when World War I ended. The jagged concrete and brick remainders of buildings now lie beneath a golf course and county park. *Author's collection.*

In the early 1960s, Kent County officials decided to speed up demolition plans because of the target shooting and the fear that children who played in cavernous rooms of the facility might be hurt. So, in 1963, a bulldozer and steel ball–swinging crane leveled the ruins and buried them.

Now lying beneath the recreation area are the broken pieces of these structures: four picric buildings (two of them completed); two nitric acid buildings; four nitrate bay storage buildings, each consisting of thirteen bays; eight magazine buildings; a main office; a carpenter and mason shop; a machine shop; a storehouse; and a laboratory. The foundation for a powerhouse also had been laid, and a 225-foot smokestack had been completed while another had been built to a height of more than 100 feet before construction halted.

Before the golf course and park were developed, several other uses of the site were considered. In 1919, the property was inspected by Governor Albert E. Sleeper and a group of legislators who were considering it for the manufacture of fertilizer, utilizing convict labor. But the governor decided against recommending the plan.

Henry Ford was said to have been interested in purchase of the property in the early 1920s; some contended that Grand Rapids industrialists blocked the move because of concern that a Ford plant would raise wage levels and take away many of their skilled workers.

In the early 1960s, civil defense officials considered using some of the ruins of the picric acid plant for possible shelter in the event of a nuclear attack.

A military atmosphere still prevails over part of the site. When the National Guard's Grand Rapids Armory was leveled in the early 1960s to make way for the I-196 freeway, a new armory was built on Forty-fourth Street at the edge of the picric acid plant site.

## A Close-Knit Group

Some were proud that they helped produce what was called "the world's most renowned underwear." Others were just glad to have a job, especially one with good conditions and friendly companions. They were women of the workforce of the old Globe Knitting Works, which was sprawled along Goodrich Street between Commerce and Ionia Avenues in downtown Grand Rapids.

For the city's women who were looking for work outside the home a century ago, it was *the* place to go. After all, most girls of those days knew a good deal about knitting. The work wasn't overly strenuous. The pay was appropriate. Trolleys provided transportation from outlying areas of the city and suburbs. And the association with other young women who had the same interests and problems contributed to camaraderie.

So, during the last few years of the nineteenth century and the first half of the twentieth, the company provided employment for hundreds, including several men in addition to the women. Today, as Globe Apartments, the renovated building offers living accommodations at the heart of the central city.

Globe Knitting Works came into being in 1897 soon after Eilert Alfred Clements, a Norwegian immigrant, went to Chicago to visit a former employer at the Princess Knitting Company. When he arrived, the building was in flames, and he helped carry out some of the equipment. The owner sold him three of the knitting machines that were salvaged, and he took them to Grand Rapids, where he installed them on the fourth floor of a building on Pearl Street, just west of Monroe Avenue.

After buying sewing machines and other necessary equipment, he was ready to start work. Without other fabric handy, he removed his undershirt and put it under the needles to knit the first item to be produced by Globe Knitting. You might say the company started "on a shirttail." At the beginning, Clements did the knitting himself, but he soon hired eight women to assist in production. He also had a salesman and another man for boxing, billing and shipping.

Unlike earlier undergarments, Globe's products offered improved comfort and appearance that was accomplished by cutting and sewing the fabric to fit the body. When the company's salesman showed samples to the purchaser at Voight-Herpolsheimer Company and asked if he'd be able to sell them, he was told that if they could be produced in quantity, the store would take all that Globe could make.

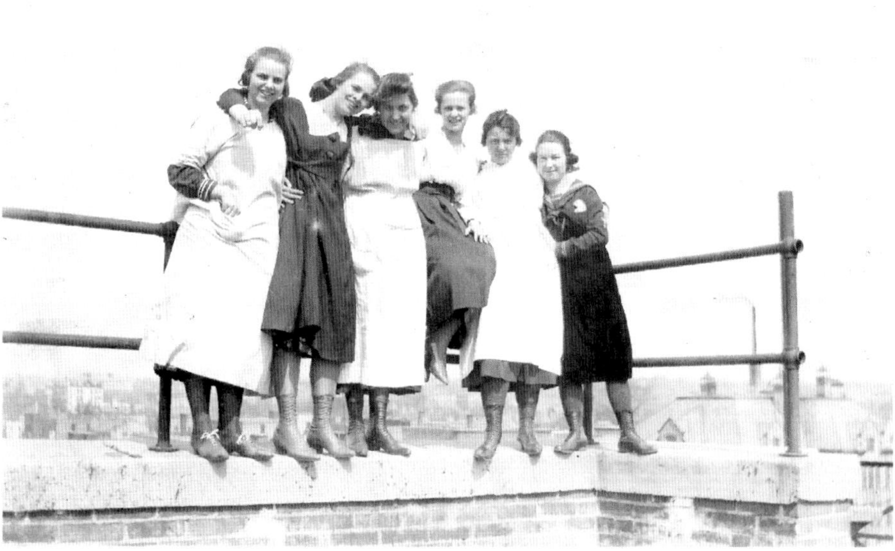

Globe Knitting Works a century ago was a popular place of employment for young Grand Rapids women, who sometimes went to the roof of the building to enjoy fresh air and sunshine during their lunch breaks.

Business began to boom, and the company moved to the Goodrich-Commerce location after building a three-and-a-half-story building there in 1900. A five-story addition was constructed in 1910, and the other section was raised to four stories. In 1917, a seven-story addition expanded the plant to Ionia Street. Another floor was added to the southeast side of the building in 1928.

Globe produced clothing for the army and navy during both world wars, though the company's workforce was diminished by employees leaving for military service: 28 men left to serve in World War I, and during World War II, 6 women and 118 men joined the armed forces.

With the labor shortage caused by World War II, Globe stepped up efforts to recruit women and produced a slick brochure. "At this time," the publication said, "we have openings for girls and women in practically all our hosiery and underwear manufacturing departments. We would like you to come in and talk with us."

Several benefits were listed on another page:

- *Clean and wholesome surroundings.*
- *Rest periods: one in the morning and one in the afternoon.*
- *Vacation with pay.*
- *Health insurance at no cost to you.*
- *An opportunity to buy your own lingerie, underwear, and hosiery at wholesale prices.*

Even in earlier days, the company had a sunny dining room and cafeteria for employees. The roof of the building was also an attraction for many of the young ladies, who enjoyed the fresh air and sunshine it offered on warm days. But all of that ended in 1952 when Globe was sold and its operations were moved to the South.

## Tower at City Center

Though it has been eclipsed by higher structures in recent years, McKay Tower at the heart of Grand Rapids was the city's tallest building for more than a half century. Built in two stages—the first four stories in 1915–16 and twelve more a decade later—it was originally the home of the Grand Rapids National City Bank and the City Trust and Savings Bank.

From 1926, when it reached sixteen stories, until the erection of the twenty-nine-story tower of the Amway Grand Plaza Hotel in 1981, McKay Tower dominated the Grand Rapids skyline. In its shadow, thousands of the city's citizens gathered for appearances of U.S. presidents and other special events. At night, the bright-red dome shining at its top was visible for miles.

It all began in 1911 when the National City Bank added to its property at Campau Square by purchasing an adjacent tract to provide a ten-thousand-square-foot building site. In its September edition that year, the *Michigan Tradesman* proclaimed, "It will ensure the harmonious and artistic treatment of the east frontage of Campau Square, which will always be the city's center."

When construction phases were completed in 1916 and again in 1926, the *Grand Rapids Herald* reminded its readers that the structure stood at a spot of historical significance. "It is pleasant to say," the paper wrote in 1916, "that Louis Campau, struck by the natural advantages of the site, here pitched his camp in conscious grandfatherhood, so to speak, of the modern metropolis."

In 1926, the *Herald* quoted historical remarks by Grand Rapids native Stewart Edward White, author of books in several genres who graduated from Central High School in 1891 and earned degrees from the University of Michigan and Columbia University. He contended that Ottawa chief Noonday should get credit for selecting the site of Grand Rapids. "And Noonday's imperial seat," he added, "was, as nearly as can be determined, on the then bank of the river where now stands the Grand Rapids National City Bank."

Upon completion of the twelve-story addition in 1926, the bank offices were located on the second floor and part of the third. Rental offices were on the rest of the third floor and those above. On the ground floor were a tearoom and cigar stand in addition to shops selling flowers, shoes, hats, jewelry and appliances. A public dining room and barbershop were in the basement. Four high-speed elevators carried clientele to their destinations.

When the bank failed during the Great Depression, the building was purchased by businessman and politician Frank D. McKay, who renamed the structure for himself. He was a three-term Michigan treasurer until 1931, when he left while a grand jury was probing his handling of state funds.

During a 1945 grand jury inquiry concerning payoffs to state legislators by lobbyists, Senator Warren G. Hooper of Albion was scheduled to testify on January 12 against McKay and others. On January 11, his body was discovered in his smoldering car on the shoulder of M-99 just north of Springport. He had been shot three times in the head.

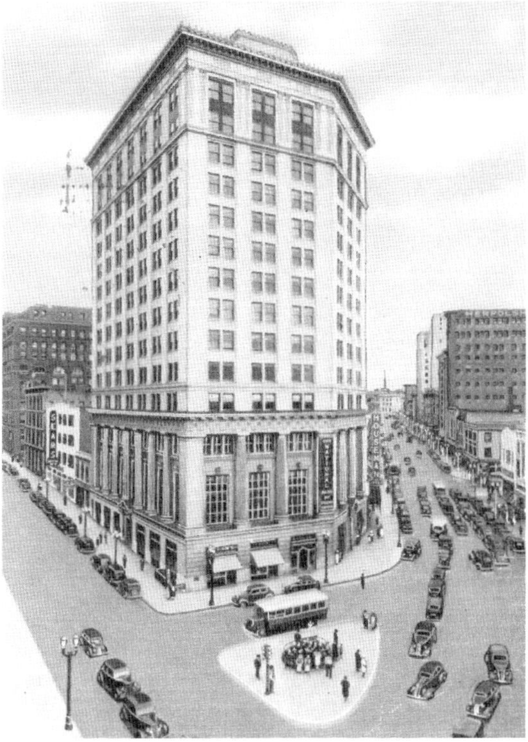

For many years, the Grand Rapids National Bank at Campau Square was the tallest building in Grand Rapids. During the Great Depression, Frank D. McKay bought the structure and named it for himself. In January 1945 a state senator was found with three bullet holes in his head the day before he was to testify against McKay before a grand jury.

The case was never solved, but the most plausible account of what happened is chronicled in the book *Three Bullets Sealed His Lips* (Michigan State University Press, 1987) by Bruce A. Rubenstein and Lawrence E. Ziewacz. They claim that McKay was able to get officials at Jackson State Prison to let inmates affiliated with Detroit's Purple Gang leave the prison in a deputy warden's car and kill Hooper, later returning to their cells.

McKay's behind-the-scenes involvement in Michigan Republican politics continued into the 1950s. His estimated wealth at the time of his death at Miami Beach in 1965 was $50 million.

## From Celebration to Calamity

A pleasant Lake Michigan beach and picturesque pier within walking distance of downtown Grand Haven have had a magnetic attraction on summertime fishermen, swimmers and sunbathers for scores of years.

In the nineteenth century, many came from Grand Rapids on Grand River steamboats, but at the outset of the 1900s, throngs began riding to the shoreline in interurban cars of the Grand Rapids, Grand Haven and Muskegon Railway. Then, soon after the interurbans brought steamboat traffic to an end, automobiles began cutting short the lives of interurban lines, and the GRGH&M was abandoned in 1928.

By then, the appealing shoreline at the mouth of Grand River had been one of Michigan's state parks for eight years, and a year later—on the Fourth of July in 1929—the largest crowd at the beach to that date basked in the sun and watched large waves crash against the shore. Forty-five thousand people were there, and eight thousand cars filled parking areas.

A few of the throng, despite the warnings of guards and bathhouse attendants, ventured into the water or walked out onto the pier. Strong winds had churned the lake for twenty-four hours, according to news reports; three men from Grand Rapids were rescued after being swept from the south pier by a huge wave at about 10:00 a.m.

Two hours later, Mildred Fifield and Marie Voight, two Grand Rapids teenagers, were walking on the pier when a ten-foot wave crashed into them. Marie grabbed a steel support and managed to stay on the pier, but Mildred was swept into the lake. Twice she swam nearly back to the pier, but more waves carried her away each time. Another victim was Frank Petruske, a champion weightlifter and swimmer from Grand Rapids, who was in chest-high water in the lake when a wave swept him away.

The body of Miss Fifield, a sixteen-year-old South High School junior whose father had been electrocuted accidentally less than a year earlier, was recovered; guards spent more than an hour trying to revive her. They had to give up and return to the treacherous lake when a large wave inundated several more persons. Some were on what news reports called a swimming plank, which was anchored two hundred feet from the shore, and others were in the water. A Coast Guard boat rescued three boys and a girl who managed to cling to the plank, but eight others sank below the waves.

Of the eight who perished, six were from Grand Rapids: Julius Tusch, nineteen; Leonard Kellogg, twenty; Robert Schindler, twenty; Walter Schwartz, nineteen; John Giddings, twenty-one; and Carl Rohloff, twenty. The other two victims were brothers from Detroit: Rudolph Pitulak, twenty-one, and Erwin Pitulak, sixteen.

Others who had come to the beach for the holiday looked on helplessly, and when news of the tragedy spread, thousands of additional motorists drove to the scene.

Bodies of only half of the victims were recovered that day. Giddings and Rudolph Pitulak were found on July 7 in the water near the pier. A day later

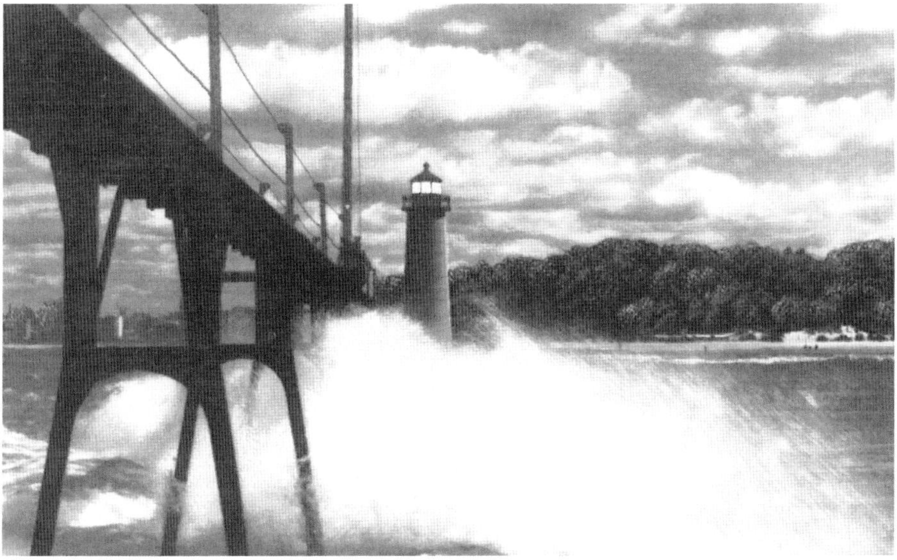

Wild waves like these crashed over the pier at Grand Haven State Park on the Fourth of July in 1929, and some of the forty-five thousand celebrating the holiday at the Lake Michigan shore ventured into the water or onto the pier despite warnings by guards. Before the day had ended, ten persons had drowned, eight of them from Grand Rapids.

the body of Schwartz was picked up by the tugboat *Louella* five miles to the northwest, and Petruske's was recovered eight miles north of Grand Haven. Last to be found was Erwin Pitulak, spotted by fishermen four miles north early on July 10. That afternoon a double funeral for the Pitulak brothers was held at Detroit.

News accounts at the time referred to the force that dragged the victims beneath the water as undertows. However, experts later pointed out that seiches likely caused the tragedy. Unlike a tsunami, which is caused by an earthquake or a meteor hitting the water, a seiche results from wind and air pressure changes that form a large wave or series of waves. Seiches are often accompanied by strong rip currents.

## When Downtown Was *the* Place

Many in the generation that preceded the baby boomers look back on the 1930s, '40s and '50s as the "glory days" of Grand Rapids. But in several respects those weren't happy years. Gloom filled the first decade as the Great Depression wiped out fortunes and jobs, only to be followed by

World War II, when thousands from Grand Rapids marched away, some never to return.

Downtown Grand Rapids, however, was a bright spot. Those were the days before malls, and downtown was where the action was. Downtown stores had the latest fashions, and its theaters showed the newest films. When dignitaries came to town, downtown is where they stayed.

Monroe Avenue was the backbone of it all. For shopping, the place to start was at one of the major department stores: Herpolsheimer's, Steketee's or Wurzburg's. They carried just about everything, and the prices were right. In January 1940, Wurzburg's had bedroom suites for $79.00 and women's three-snap boots for $1.65. At Steketee's, you could get Arnold sports shoes for $7.50, and five pastel Cannon bath towels for $1.00. Herpolsheimer's offered Bellaire sheets for $0.99 and men's worsted suits for $24.50. A few years later, at its nearby appliance store, Herps was even selling two-seat airplanes at $3,495.00.

The favorite place for kids was "Dime Store Row" in the block of Monroe between Market and Pearl Streets. Woolworth's was at the Pearl-Monroe corner, while Kresge's anchored the other end. Among the six establishments in between were two more five-and-dimes: F&W Grand and W.T. Grant. While mothers picked out hair ribbons, furniture polish and kitchen utensils, kids hovered at the toy counters examining dolls, jump ropes, lead soldiers and Big Little Books with stories and cartoons of Dick Tracy, Little Orphan Annie, Tom Mix and Flash Gordon.

There were lunch counters with tasty sandwiches and ice cream sundaes, and Kresge's sheet music department always had a pianist banging out the latest pop tunes. Nearby was one of those photo booths where you and a friend could squeeze in and get four almost-instant photos for a quarter.

There were few, if any, vacant stores on Monroe, a thoroughfare with all kinds of specialty shops. Up and down the avenue were shoe stores, drugstores, jewelry shops and even a grocery store. Attracting the ladies were many women's wear establishments such as Gantos, Sarret and Virginia Dare. Jacobson's joined them with a store in the Pantlind Hotel building in 1943 and then moved to the east end of Monroe in '54. Men waiting for their wives often headed for Goebel and Brown's sporting goods store, the United Cigar Shop, Sears Roebuck or the Camera Shop.

For families who had gone their separate ways to shop, the Pantlind's lobby was a good place to regroup. Then they might set off for clothing at Houseman and Jones, leather goods at Groskopf's or a treat at Mary Lee's Candies.

Shopping downtown usually meant a good time, but it wouldn't usually be described as exciting. Soon after the war ended in 1945, however, the *Grand*

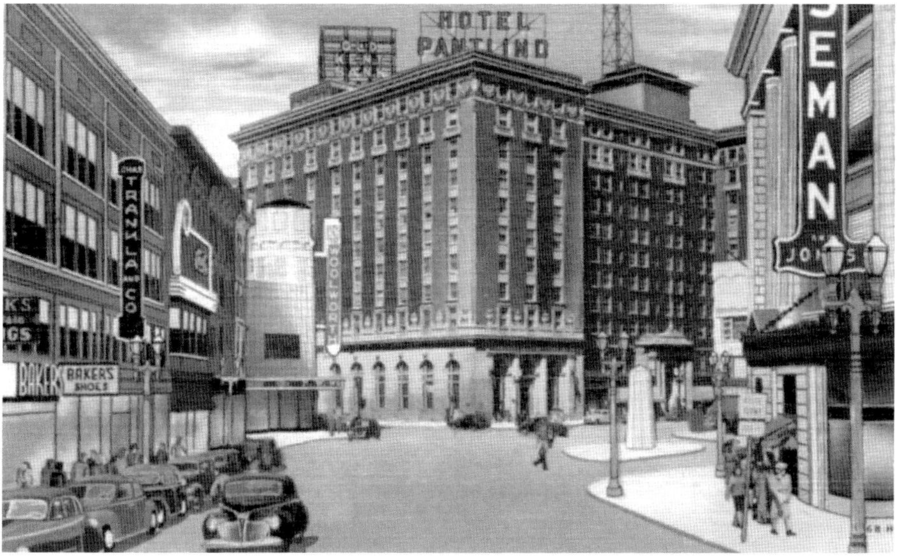


Despite the hardships of the Great Depression and World War II, many Grand Rapids residents found happiness in downtown Grand Rapids before the arrival of suburban shopping malls. Toy counters at "Dime Store Row" in this stretch of Monroe Avenue attracted local lads and lasses. Woolworth's anchored one end of the block, and Kresge's was at the other, with two more five-and-dimes in between.

*Rapids Press* carried a Houseman and Jones ad stating that six hundred white shirts would go on sale at 9:30 a.m. the next day. When the door opened, there was a near riot, requiring police intervention. The store's telephone operator, caught in the crowd, tried to wedge her way in and was slapped in the face by an irate shopper. "Who do you think you are," the woman shouted, "Houseman's daughter?"

Downtown's theaters were the place to go for first-run films. During early January 1940, the Majestic was showing *Gulliver's Travels*, while the Regent featured Deanna Durbin in *First Love*. Keith's had a live stage show, *Hooray America*, with "20 girls, 150 daring costumes, and 19 big scenes." At the Savoy, where you could usually count on a double feature, the attractions were Wallace Beery and Virginia Grey in *Thunder Afloat*, and Bing Crosby and Louise Campbell in *The Star Maker*. Ticket prices were typically eighty cents before 5:00 p.m., and forty cents after. Kids could get in for ten cents any time.

The really big attractions downtown were events like the annual Santa Claus Parade along Monroe. Civic Auditorium extravaganzas such as the Shrine Circus attracted thousands, too. And when leading political figures came to the city, downtown crowds might be in the hundreds of thousands.

Dignitaries would come by train and proceed behind bands over the few blocks from Union Station to Campau Square.

October 1936 brought a double dose of that kind of excitement less than three weeks before the presidential election. That's when President Franklin D. Roosevelt and Republican candidate Alfred M. Landon made successive Grand Rapids appearances, with Landon's train pulling out of Union Station just twenty-five minutes before Roosevelt's arrived.

Today's malls may be great places, but you're not likely to experience those kinds of thrills there. It was a glorious time for downtown.

## HATCHING WHIRLYBIRDS

It's unlikely that anyone in western Michigan had seen a helicopter before Saturday, May 26, 1945, when three specks appeared just above the eastern horizon and grew until they halted in midair above the old Kent County Airport.

These strange airships that imitated the flight of hummingbirds were incomprehensible to most. In its next edition, the *Grand Rapids Press* referred to them as "versatile craft, capable of flying a hundred miles an hour and being able to move straight up or down, forward or backward."

A few choppers had been flown in Europe as early as 1935, and in 1939 Igor Sikorsky succeeded in getting one off the ground on this side of the Atlantic. His Vought-Sikorsky-300 was the first workable helicopter that didn't need two rotors moving in opposite directions to eliminate torque. He used a tail rotor to provide thrust in the opposite direction of the torque.

In the early years of World War II, the U.S. Air Force was interested in military use of the machines and contracted with Vought-Sikorsky to produce R-4 and R-5 helicopters. Success of the R-4s led to birth of the R-6 model, which had a metal fuselage rather than one of canvas.

When the war effort required Vought-Sikorsky to concentrate on production of F4U Corsair fighter planes for the U.S. Navy and Marine Corps, the company agreed to license production of R-6s to the Kelvinator Division of Nash-Kelvinator Corporation. Major parts of these helicopters were made at the huge Kelvinator refrigerator plant on Clyde Park Avenue at the west edge of Grand Rapids. Then they were shipped to Detroit for assembly.

The men and women who produced more than half the helicopters delivered to Allied forces during the war didn't get to see the finished product until those three specks moved in, hovered above them and then landed on

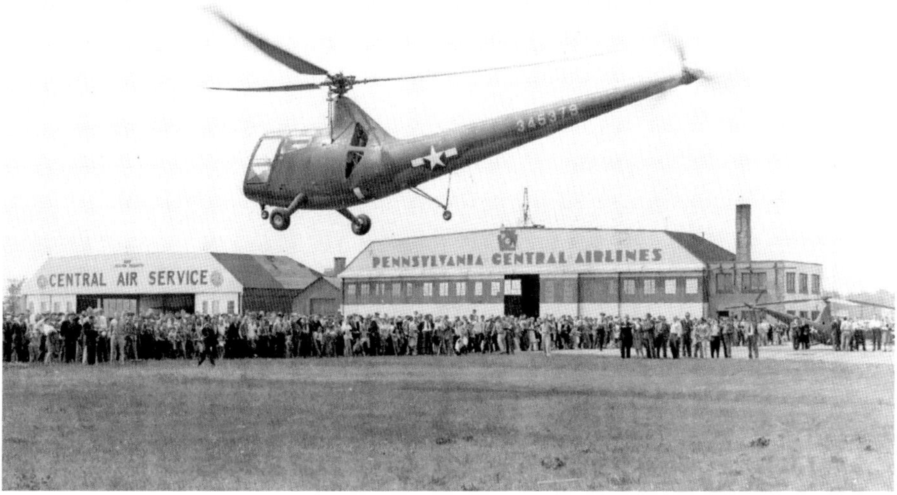


Nash-Kelvinator employees who produced major parts for more than half of the helicopters made in America for use by Allied forces during World War II never saw one of the completed airships until May 26, 1945. The parts were shipped to Detroit, where they were assembled, and three of the choppers were flown to Kent County Airport that day to show the workers what they'd been building. *Given to author by* Grand Rapids Press *photographer Earl Spielmacher.*

the airfield apron at Thirty-second Street and Madison Avenue. Before they returned to Detroit, they provided thrills for a few of the Grand Rapids plant's employees by inviting them into the cockpit and lifting them several feet into the air.

According to one of Vought-Sikorsky's engineers, production at Grand Rapids was a bit unorthodox at times. When supplies of minor parts such as fasteners were depleted, he said, Kelvinator employees would get substitutes at local hardware stores. Two of them were conveniently located—Jelsema's Hardware, directly across Clyde Park Avenue from the factory's main entrance, and Groen's Hardware, adjacent to the plant at the corner of Clyde Park and Grandville Avenues.

Though some of Vought-Sikorsky's experts referred to the helicopters made with Grand Rapids parts as "Kelvicopters" and "Refrigerotors," they were impressed by Kelvinator's speed in turning out the choppers. They pointed out that parts were made at twice the monthly rate required by the contract.

Some of the R-6s were fitted with capsules on each side of the fuselage to carry litters for medical evacuation, and some had floats for operation from water. A few had racks for bombs and depth charges for use against ground forces, ships and submarines. However, their principal use in World War II was for observation and liaison purposes.

All the helicopters manufactured in the United States for Allied forces during the war were Sikorsky models—128 R-4s, 65 R-5s and 219 R-6s. The 219 R-6s manufactured by Nash-Kelvinator accounted for more than half of the total of 412 choppers. When the war ended, 205 more R-6s that Nash-Kelvinator had produced were accepted by the army and shipped to Randolph Field, Texas, for storage. Eventually, they were scrapped after rust and deterioration made them useless.

## Girls and Diamonds

Any Grand Rapids girl of the early 1940s who hoped to earn a living as an athlete would have been considered a wild dreamer.

To be sure, many women began working outside the home during World War II. But professional sports? Forget it. Such things just didn't happen, at least not until 1945, when the Grand Rapids Chicks came to town. These Chicks were baseball players—female baseball players. And they really could play the game—better, in fact, than a lot of men.

The Chicks were one of six teams in the All-American Girls Professional Baseball League when they moved to Grand Rapids from Milwaukee in 1945. The league had been established in 1943 by Chicago Cubs owner Philip K. Wrigley, who feared that the loss of many major-league players to the war effort might empty ballparks.

League teams during the first season were the Racine Belles and Kenosha Comets from Wisconsin, the Rockford (Illinois) Peaches and the South Bend (Indiana) Blue Sox. Milwaukee and Minneapolis fielded teams in 1944, but the sport didn't catch on in either city. A year later, Milwaukee's Chicks relocated in Grand Rapids, and the Minneapolis team moved to Fort Wayne. The exploits of the teams were fictionalized in the 1992 movie *A League of Their Own* starring Tom Hanks, Madonna, Geena Davis and Rosie O'Donnell.

Possibly the most enthusiastic fan in Grand Rapids was ten-year-old Marilyn Jenkins. To pay her way into the games at South Field (the same place where President Gerald R. Ford played high school football but now just an empty field along Cottage Grove Street between Jefferson and Madison Avenues), she got a job picking up trash on the diamond and beneath the stands. During her early teens, she became the Chicks' batgirl, and she dreamed of one day playing on the team.

The Chicks turned out to be one of the league's best franchises. Attendance was good in Grand Rapids, and the team was the only one in the league to make the season-ending playoffs every year. Grand Rapids was the playoff champion in 1947 and 1953 and won the regular season championship in 1948.

After the war, however, fan interest in women's baseball waned as major-league baseball revived; television also brought baseball and other entertainment right into homes. Marilyn Jenkins's dream came true during that period, when she began playing for the Chicks as a catcher in 1952 at the tender age of seventeen. Financial difficulties began forcing teams to disband, and 1954 was the Chicks' last season. Jenkins could see the handwriting on the wall when her pay was counted out in one-dollar bills.

Her last game—and the team's—was the first game of what was supposed to be a three-game series in the '54 playoffs. The Chicks were hosting the Fort Wayne Daisies at South Field. During pregame warm-ups, Chicks manager Woody English discovered that the Daisies were planning to use Ruth Richards of the Rockford Peaches as catcher. English protested that she was ineligible (since she was on another team). The argument was settled with an agreement that the game would be played under protest and the matter resolved before the next game. The Chicks won the first contest, 8–7, scoring the winning run after two outs in the ninth inning.

At Fort Wayne the next day, when the Chicks found Richards in the lineup again, English ordered his team off the field. He ended up in a fistfight with Daisy manager Bill Allington, and when umpires pulled the two apart, Grand Rapids forfeited the game—and the series—to Fort Wayne because the Chicks had left the field.

The Grand Rapids team never played again. The league's diamonds and grandstands were empty. It was a sad ending to ten years of thrills for Chicks players and thousands of their fans.

## Fan Favorites

Regulars in the stands at South Field loved their Chicks, and many focused their adoration on just a single athlete. Among the most popular were Alma Ziegler, Connie Wisniewski and Ruth Lessing.

Ziegler, whose two nicknames were "Ziggy" and "Gabby," is the only player who was with the team for all of its eleven seasons; she was the squad's captain during all of them. Fans loved her fiery and acrobatic performances at second base, and after the first four years, she also worked on the mound. In 1950, when she was the AAGPBL's Player of the Year, the crowd at one game gave her a standing ovation and showered her with gifts. The following year, she was the league's pitching champion, and during the next two seasons, she was an all-star selection.

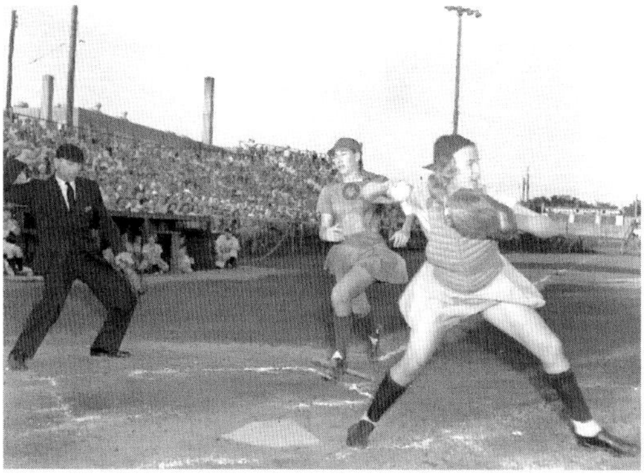

Wisniewski, tabbed by the press as the "Iron Woman," was also a stellar pitcher who switched to the outfield after underhand pitching was no longer the league's modus operandi. She was the AAGPBL's Player of the Year in 1945 when she won thirty-two games and lost only eleven. During that season, she registered a phenomenal earned run average of 0.81; in one doubleheader she pitched, and won, both games. Her record was even better the following year when she hurled forty-six complete games without relief, winning thirty-three and losing only nine. She was an all-star selection in 1946, '48, '51 and '52.

*Inset above*: Chicks catcher "Tex" Lessing fires the ball to first base after a bases-loaded forced out at home plate, ending a Kenosha rally at South Field in 1948. During another game, she slugged an umpire when he made a call she didn't like. She was fined $100 by the league, but Grand Rapids fans gave her $2,000. She paid the fine, gave the rest to charity and apologized to the ump. *Courtesy of Grand Rapids History and Special Collections, Archives, Grand Rapids Public Library.*

Lessing, known to Grand Rapids fans as "Tex," was a standout behind home plate for the Chicks from 1946 to 1949. Attractive but tough, she was pictured in early league promotional materials to demonstrate players' feminine appeal as well as athletic ability. But she wasn't so sweet on the field of play. In a game between Grand Rapids and Racine, she disagreed with a call by the plate umpire and tore into him with fists flying. The league fined her $100, but fans rushed to her aid with supporting gifts of $2,000. She paid the fine and donated the rest of the money to charity. Later she sent a letter of apology to the ump, and the two became close friends.

## GR's Circle-C Cowboys

Forty-two of us in the lobby of the Grand Rapids National City Bank at Campau Square at 6:00 a.m. on March 4, 1946, knew where we were going. After boarding a bus, the next stop for our gang of eighteen-year-olds would be the East Jefferson Recruiting Station in Detroit where we'd become members of the U.S. armed forces.

Our itinerary after the Detroit stop, however, was a mystery. The guns of World War II had fallen silent six months before, but military conscription continued, particularly to provide manpower for occupation forces.

After being sworn in at Detroit, most of us were sent to Fort Sheridan, Illinois, where we were issued uniforms, introduced to army life and presented with orders for training or service. In my pocket when I boarded the bus at Grand Rapids was a "to whom it may concern" letter from Lee Woodruff, editor of the *Grand Rapids Press*, suggesting that I be assigned to the staff of a military newspaper such as *Stars and Stripes*. But it didn't impress Fort Sheridan's placement people, who sent me to Camp Joseph T. Robinson in Arkansas to become a rifleman.

After completing basic training and sailing to Germany aboard the USS *Kokomo Victory*, I pulled the letter out of my pocket again at the Army Replacement Depot in Marburg. No one was impressed there either.

At Marburg we learned about the U.S. Constabulary, a new mechanized force being organized to maintain military and civilian security and to control borders of the American Zone of Occupation. Its troopers would patrol every town in the zone, hunting for Germans and displaced persons suspected of smuggling, black marketeering or possessing weapons. The

Constabulary also would establish border checkpoints and keep an eye on other GIs for disciplinary and traffic violations in addition to crimes against civilians. Furthermore, its troopers would be prepared to respond quickly to riots, uprisings or other threats to security of U.S. forces in the zone.

Just a limited number of lucky applicants would be considered for this impressive new police force, we were told. By this time, however, I'd been in the army long enough to know that volunteering isn't usually a good idea. None of my acquaintances signed up to join the army's new elite unit, but after a week at Marburg, most of us were in trains headed for Constabulary bases.

Among those destined to become Constabulary troopers were John Katerburg and John Vander Ley, two Grand Rapids men I met at Campau Square the morning our adventure began. We were together at Fort Sheridan, Camp Robinson, on the *Kokomo Victory* and at Marburg. But now we went to separate Constabulary squadrons.

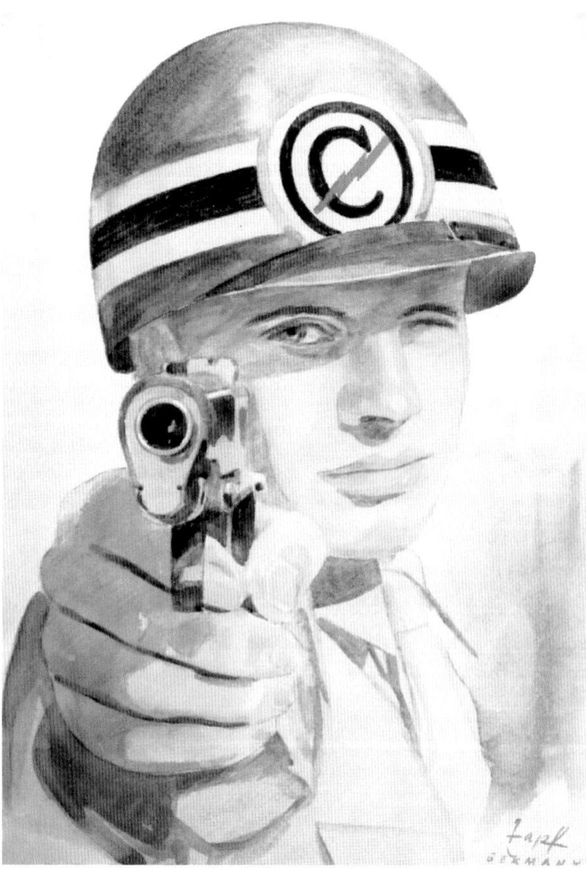

Grand Rapids troopers serving with the army's U.S. Constabulary in the occupation of Germany after World War II wore helmets with the unit's colorful Circle-C emblem. The same symbol adorned the vehicles they used on patrols. As a police unit, the Constabulary had jurisdiction over civilians as well as military personnel and was prepared to respond quickly to security threats.

My train took me south to the foothills of the Bavarian Alps, where I served as a clerk typist/investigator in the intelligence section of the Sixty-sixth Constabulary Squadron based at Fort May, a former German Army Camp in the village of Degerndorf. The Sixty-sixth Squadron policed six counties in the southeastern corner of Germany and patrolled a long stretch of the border along the Inn River, which flowed between Germany and the American and French zones of Austria.

The Constabulary, it turned out, was a real spit-and-polish outfit, designed to impress German civilians who called its troopers *der Blitzpolezei* (the Lightning Police). Other GIs branded them "Circle-C Cowboys," a rather disparaging reference to the unit's insignia—a yellow disk with a large blue "C" pierced by a red lightning bolt and centered in a blue circle.

The symbol seemed everywhere—on the troopers' shoulder patches, at the front of their on-duty helmet liners and on their jeeps, M-8 armored cars, trucks and tanks. The helmet liners and vehicles also were circled by two broad stripes of yellow and blue.

Those of us who policed Germany after World War II rarely experienced the insecurity that has confronted U.S. soldiers in twenty-first century occupations. I was unarmed when off duty and off the base, whether alone or in a group. Although I always carried a .45-caliber pistol while on duty beyond the walls of our base, the gun wasn't loaded. With an empty clip inserted, no one could tell whether the weapon contained bullets or not. But it would have been worthless as a weapon unless swung as a club or hurled as a missile. Unlike Barney Fife of Mayberry fame, I didn't even have a bullet in my pocket.

## Riding the Pere Marquette

Luxury and comfort came to the rails between Grand Rapids and Detroit in August 1946 when two diesel-powered streamlined trains replaced the humdrum cars and steam locomotives that had carried passengers between the two largest of Michigan's cities for the better part of a century.

Operated by the Pere Marquette Railroad, which then was controlled by the Chesapeake and Ohio Railroad and a year later formally merged with the larger line, the two diesels with seven-car train sets provided three round trips between the cities each day and cut forty minutes off the previous fastest time for the run.

After the merger, though the railroad was the Chesapeake and Ohio, the streamliners retained the Pere Marquette name. With fluted strips of stainless steel and brilliant blue and yellow paint, emulating University of Michigan colors, the locomotives and cars of the Pere Marquette streamliners were dazzling.

Four days before the beginning of regular service on August 10, 1946, a promotional run carried newsmen and dignitaries from Grand Rapids and Lansing to Detroit. Also aboard was sixteen-year-old Joan Kelly, daughter of Governor Harry J. Kelly, who christened one of the locomotives with a bottle of comingled water from the Grand and Detroit Rivers.

Riders of the train were impressed by its exterior and interior beauty in addition to the comfort and smoothness of the ride. All its components were made after World War II, making it America's first postwar streamliner. Injectors for engines of the two locomotives were made by the Electro-Motive Division of General Motors at its Diesel Equipment Division in suburban Grand Rapids.

Behind the locomotive of each train were a mail car, a baggage car, a forty-four-seat diner, two coaches with fifty-four seats, a coach with fifty-six seats and observation windows facing rearward and a coach with fifty-eight seats and observation windows looking ahead. The seats were Heywood-Wakefield Company's new "Sleepy Hollow" design, which could be adjusted to ten different reclining positions. Passengers also could leave their regular seats and congregate in ten-chair lounge areas of each coach.

Besides overhead lights in the cars, there were two reading lights above each seat, one directed to the window seat and the other to the seat at the aisle. Bulkheads at ends of the cars featured circular mirrors or large photographs of country scenes on the PM route. Women's powder rooms had an alcove with an easy chair and a wraparound three-sided mirror.

The dining car of each train was especially appealing. Placement of the kitchen at the middle of the car, rather than at one end, provided two cozier dining areas instead of the typical long one of earlier trains. Diagonal seating at triangular and rectangular tables set into alcoves along the walls permitted serving from between the tables, leaving the aisle free and providing more privacy.

Most servers on earlier trains had been male stewards, but those in the new Pere Marquette diners were women, known as "dining car hostesses." All were high school graduates between twenty and thirty years old, and all were from Grand Rapids.

The trains made the Grand Rapids–Detroit run in two hours and forty minutes. Buses at that time usually took four hours and thirty minutes.

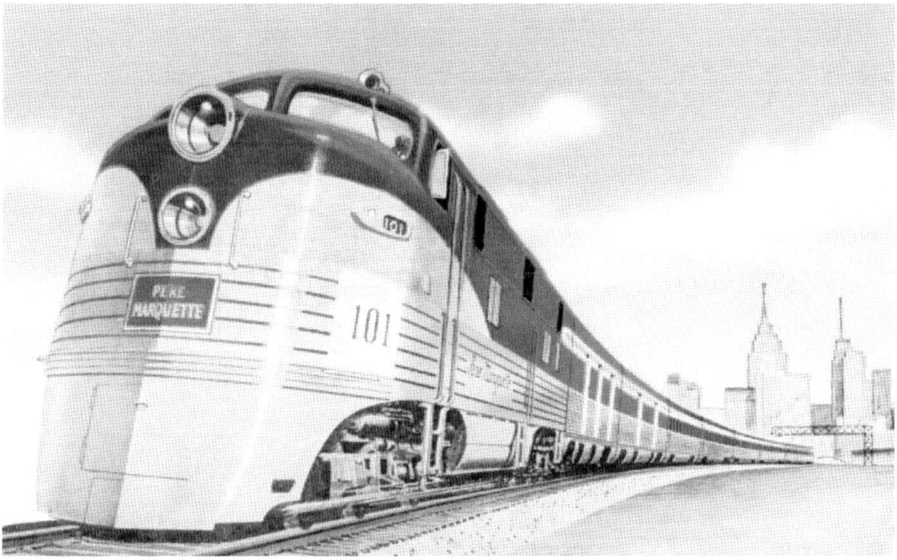

America's first postwar streamliner went into service between Grand Rapids and Detroit in August 1946. The sleek locomotives and cars were decorated with fluted stainless steel strips and bright blue and yellow paint. The new trains cut forty minutes off the time for the trip, and passengers were impressed by the comfort as well as the speed of the trains.

In 1948 success of the initial Pere Marquettes prompted C&O to begin streamliner service between Grand Rapids and Chicago, with a connecting service between Holland and Muskegon. A year later, the railroad put a similar train into operation between Detroit and Saginaw.

Arrival of the streamliners boosted patronage initially, but in subsequent years, passenger counts dropped steadily, and by 1970 most of the once-popular trains operated with only a single coach behind the locomotive. The C&O's passenger service in Michigan halted at the end of April 1971. In 1984, however, Amtrak revived service between Grand Rapids and Chicago with a train appropriately named the Pere Marquette.

## Fishing Wasn't Great—Just Okay

When fish aren't biting, conversation in a rowboat generally doesn't produce spectacular results. But when two fishing buddies, both south-side school superintendents, started talking about high school sports during a lull in angling action half a century ago, they came up with an idea that generated what has become Michigan's largest athletic conference.

It's known as the OK, or Ottawa-Kent, Conference, so named because its first members were from those counties. Founded in 1957, the conference began competition a year later with just five schools. But in 2008, when the seven Grand Rapids City League schools began OK competition, the conference had representatives in seven counties: thirty in Kent; eleven in Ottawa, three each in Allegan and Muskegon; two in Barry; and one each in Ionia and Belding. Acceptance of the Grand Rapids schools boosted conference membership to fifty-one for 2008–9 competition, the OK's fifty-first.

The two men on that 1950s fishing expedition didn't dream that their brainstorm would become something that big. All they wanted was for their students to compete in a league that offered balanced competition, with schools of comparable size competing against one another.

One of the men was the late Russell "Rud" Formsma, superintendent of Kelloggsville Public Schools, whose teams had played as independents since withdrawing from the Bar-Ken-Al League in 1949. His fishing buddy, the late Albert Deal, was head man at Rogers Public Schools, a Bar-Ken-Al member that had been a twelve-grade school system for only two years.

As they began to explore the possibility of establishing a new league, Lee High School withdrew from the Grand Valley Conference. As one of the

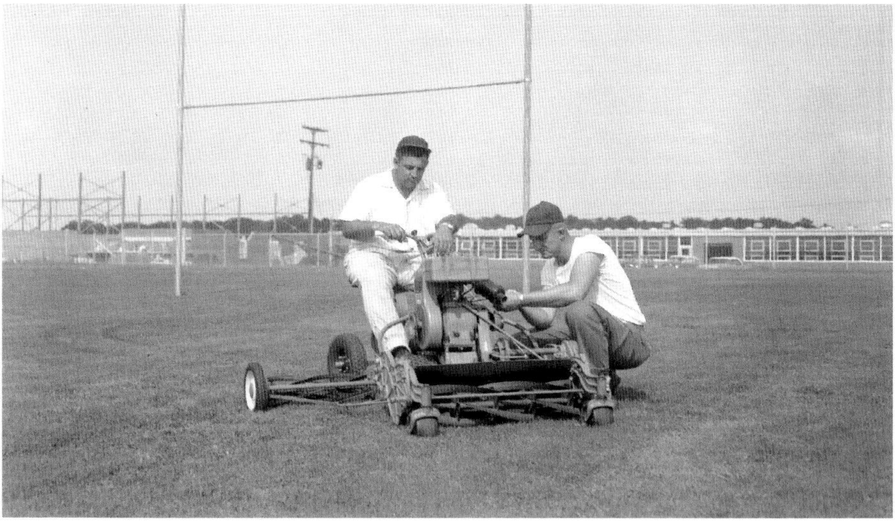

Groundskeepers at Rogers High School in suburban Wyoming concentrated in 1958 on getting the field in shape for their football team's first competition in the new OK Conference. Rogers edged Kelloggsville in the final game of the season to capture the OK's first championship. *Courtesy of Grand Rapids History and Special Collections, Archives, Grand Rapids Public Library.*

smallest schools in the Grand Rapids area, Lee had been a tough competitor against the six larger schools of the Grand Valley for twenty-three years. Only East Grand Rapids and Godwin Heights, then the Grand Valley's two largest schools, had won more conference championships than Lee. East and Godwin each had twenty-two trophies and Lee fifteen.

But on January 27, 1957, the numerically disadvantaged Rebels withdrew from the league. Less than two months later, representatives from Lee, Kelloggsville and Rogers met with officials of two other districts—Byron Center and Hudsonville—to finalize formation of a new conference. Byron Center and Hudsonville announced decisions to terminate their other league affiliations at the meeting, and the five schools developed plans for a new league that would begin competition in the fall of 1958.

Before then a sixth school, Forest Hills, was admitted to the conference, though it didn't take part in OK action until the 1960 spring sports season after it became a twelve-grade school system. In the opening OK competition, football in 1958, Rogers nipped Kelloggsville in the final game to take the first OK championship.

During its first half century, teams from the OK captured 226 state championships—118 by girls competing in thirteen sports, and 108 by boys in fifteen sports. The girls held that slight edge even though the boys had much earlier opportunities. State basketball tournaments for young men began in 1917, while the first tournaments for girls were in 1973 after passage of Title IX.

OK teams obviously have had more than their share of success. Of greater importance, however, is that thousands of girls and boys in Grand Rapids–area schools have enjoyed thrills and benefited from character-building experiences.

Who'd have thought that all of that would have been generated in a rowboat on a west Michigan lake?

## Finding a Home for GVSU

Half a century ago, the search for what is now the campus of Grand Valley State University triggered a dash by twenty west Michigan communities to get in line for consideration. Governor G. Mennen Williams in 1960 had appointed a board of control and signed legislation authorizing it to secure a site, and the search intensified early in 1961.

The proposed four-year Grand Valley College was intended principally to serve students in Allegan, Barry, Ionia, Kent, Montcalm, Muskegon, Newaygo and Ottawa Counties. A Citizens Advisory Council of about one hundred representatives from those counties was organized to help bring the dream to reality, and in January 1961 its Site Selection Committee began soliciting proposals. As they rolled in, committee members visited the sites, held public hearings to get citizen input and reviewed data with professional consultants.

The list of twenty contenders began to shrink as the committee compared their attributes with its required criteria: proximity to a major highway and the population center of the eight counties, size of three hundred to six hundred acres, water supply and natural beauty. Among proposed sites still in contention after the initial cuts were the following:

- Aman Park—324.0 acres owned by the City of Grand Rapids. It could be expanded with 162.5 additional acres, for which commitments had been obtained.
- Allendale—400 acres two miles west of Aman Park on the south side of Highway M50 (now M45) and the west bank of Grand River.
- Marne—364 acres twelve miles from downtown Grand Rapids. It was north of Johnson Street between Twenty-fourth and Thirty-second Avenues.
- Palmer Park, Wyoming—360 acres with ruins of a never-completed industrial complex that would have produced picric acid for use in World War I. It's now the site of Palmer Park, Leonard E. Kaufmann Golf Course and the National Guard Armory.
- Cannonsburg Road—100 acres, with additional land available. It was on both sides of Cannonsburg Road on the north shore of Grand River east of Blythefield Country Club.
- Downtown Grand Rapids—A site bounded by Division and Bond Avenues and Lyon and Michigan Streets. The proposal envisioned a thirteen-story building for most college operations.
- Grand Haven—400 acres near the Ottawa-Muskegon county line, with 1,500 feet of frontage on Lake Michigan. It was north of North Shore Drive, west of Dogwood Drive and south of Hickory Street.
- Lowell—447 acres of the Lowell State Game Area northeast of Lowell. Proponents said that it and an adjacent piece of about the same size in Ionia County could be transferred without cost by the state.

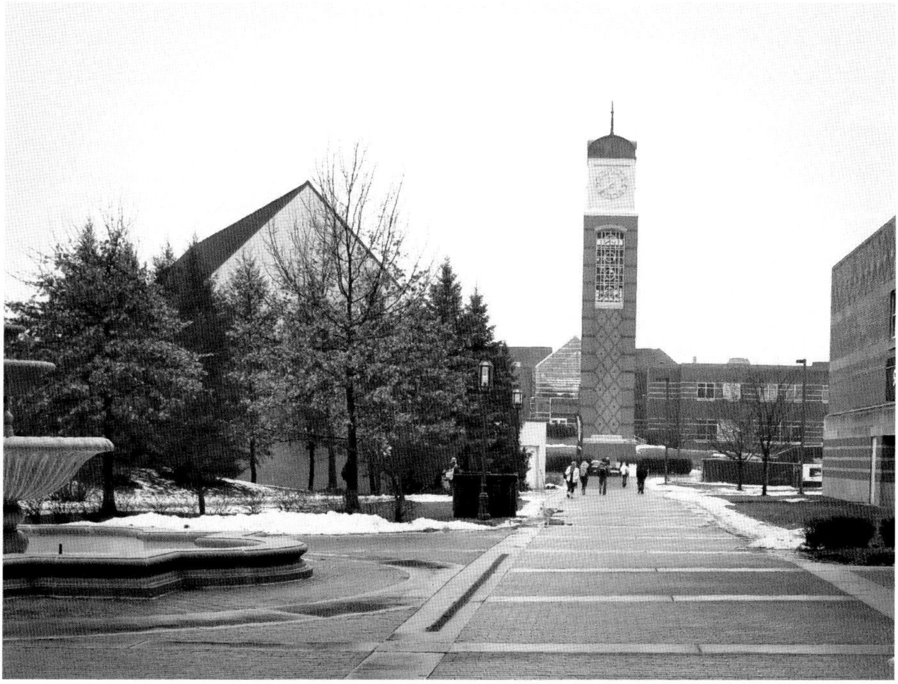

When planners of a new state college hunted for a site for the institution in the early 1960s, twenty communities submitted proposals describing the advantages of their locations. Allendale in northern Ottawa County came closest to meeting requirements of the site selection committee, and a four-hundred-acre tract there became Grand Valley State College. Now known as Grand Valley State University, this is how it looks today. *Courtesy of Jeton Grajqevci, a Grand Valley student.*

- Muskegon—800 acres bounded by the Muskegon River at the north; Marquette Avenue, south; US-31, west; and Sheridan Drive, east.
- Rockford—900 acres with boundaries of 11-Mile Road on the north; 10 Mile Road, south; Courtland Drive, west; and Shaner Avenue, east.

In mid-February, the Site Selection Committee announced the final five sites being considered. Two of them—Allendale and Marne—were close to the projected population center of the eight counties. Three—Grand Haven, Muskegon and Rockford—were at the perimeter of the area. The committee recommended that the board of control select either the Allendale or Marne site, and on April 7 the board announced that Allendale would be the location of the new college.

Groundbreaking for construction of the first building on the campus was scheduled for August 28, 1962, with the dirt to be moved by dynamite rather than shovels. Governor John B. Swainson pushed a button to set off the blast, but nothing happened. He tried again and again but finally gave up. David Dutcher, the master of ceremonies, announced, "Let us consider the ground broken," and the ceremony concluded. Then, as the crowd dispersed, a tremendous explosion brought cheers and a propitious beginning for the college.

## A Refuge from Vietnam

The hearts and doors of Grand Rapids opened wide to refugees from war-torn southeast Asia in the mid-1970s, thanks in large measure to a local clergyman and his wife, hundreds of ordinary but compassionate citizens and the late president Gerald R. Ford.

In 1975 Reverend Howard Schipper, pastor of Bethany Reformed Church, and his wife, Marybelle, were flying home from a conference at Robert H. Schuller's Crystal Cathedral in Garden Grove, California. At the conference, they heard Schuller urge, "If you want your church to be successful and have some impact, find a need and fill it."

With the Schippers on their return flight to Michigan were several orphaned Vietnamese children who, after having survived a plane crash in Vietnam a few weeks earlier, were being escorted to Boston by Catholic nuns. Howard and Marybelle realized that they had found their need. As they flew home, they pondered what Christians in the United States could do to help.

Meanwhile, soon after taking the nation's highest office in 1974, President Ford encountered opposition in Congress and among the general public to his effort to extend a helping hand to refugees. Ford's former press secretary, Ron Nessen, later recalled showing Ford a news report concerning rejection by the House of Representatives of a bill that would have provided funds to resettle thousands of south Vietnamese refugees facing imprisonment and possible execution.

"I'd never heard Ford curse before," Nessen wrote in a December 2006 *Washington Post* article, "but he did that day when he read the story." Ford undertook a public lobbying campaign, including visits to refugee camps in Arkansas and Florida, which turned around public and Congressional opposition to helping the refugees. "It was his greatest display of moral leadership."

Shortly thereafter, Dr. William Ver Meulen and his wife, Wilma, members of Bethany Reformed, attended a State Department dinner in Washington,

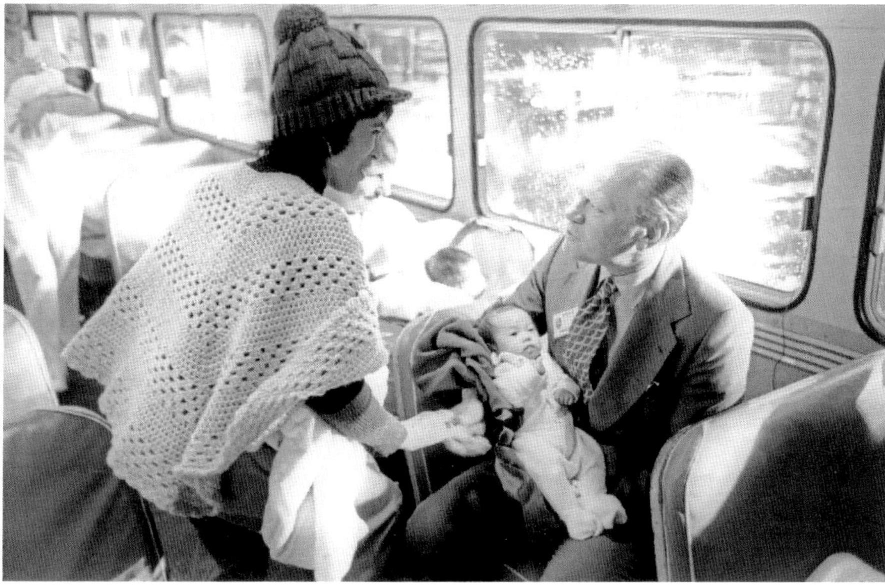

Seated on a bus at a California air force base in 1975, President Gerald R. Ford offers encouragement to a Vietnamese lady while holding her baby. With his help a Grand Rapids church brought fugitives from Vietnam to Grand Rapids, and that led to establishment of an agency that resettled eleven thousand refugees in west Michigan during the next twenty-four years. *Courtesy of Gerald R. Ford Library.*

D.C., at the invitation of President and Mrs. Ford. Contacts the Ver Meulens were able to make at the State Department cleared the way for support of an effort to resettle up to one hundred refugee families in west Michigan.

The Schippers initially hoped to bring one plane load of refugees to Grand Rapids with the help of area churches. They would call the venture "Freedom Flight." They presented their idea to the congregation, and members of a Sunday school class began contacting members of other churches for support. Leadership from the Catholic Human Development Office and an emerging local branch of Church World Service were at the forefront of the effort.

As the war in Vietnam was nearing an end, Ford ordered American naval and contract vessels to assist in the evacuation of refugees from coastal seaports. He initiated a program to provide temporary housing for refugees at four reception centers in the United States. Thousands of Vietnamese processed at the centers prepared to be resettled in every state of the nation.

Much of the American public, however, was not enthusiastic about welcoming the Vietnamese. A spokesperson for the State of Michigan said at the time that the sympathetic reception for Vietnamese orphans did not apply to Vietnamese adults.

Positive attitudes prevailed in Grand Rapids, however. Reverend Schipper traveled to Fort Chaffee in Arkansas to select the first refugees to be settled in this area. Meanwhile, Grand Rapids Public Schools superintendent Philip Runkel formed a coalition of one hundred representatives from industry, labor, the Red Cross, volunteer agencies and other organizations to develop plans concerning how the community could help.

With leadership from the school system's bilingual education and adult education departments, English classes for the arriving refugees were offered, first at Bethany Reformed and subsequently at other locations.

From that coalition, eighteen representatives were selected to form what was known as the Freedom Flight Task Force. The operational arm of the task force became the Freedom Flight Refugee Center, which continued as a Church World Service affiliate, bringing refugees to west Michigan for the next twenty-four years.

Reverend Schipper, who headed the initial task force, and his wife supervised activities of the refugee center until it was closed in 1999. By that time, it had resettled more than eleven thousand refugees from southeast Asia and other parts of the world in the Grand Rapids area.

In addition to his leadership at Freedom Flight, Reverend Schipper continued to serve as pastor of Bethany Reformed and, later, as general secretary of the Michigan Synod of the Reformed Church in America. His death in 2006 saddened the thousands of Vietnamese who had come to this area as a result of his compassion and devotion. President Ford's passing added to the grief yet also served as a reminder of the extraordinary compassion of the most famous Grand Rapids citizen.

"Throughout the final ordeal of Indochina, Gerald Ford focused on America's duty to rescue the maximum number of those who had relied on us," former secretary of state Henry A. Kissinger commented in a eulogy for Ford. "The extraction of 150,000 refugees was the consequence. And, typically, Gerald Ford saw it as his duty to visit one of the refugee camps long after public attention had moved elsewhere."

Also typical of Ford was his deflection of the credit to the citizenry. He said at the time, "The warmth and generosity that have characterized the welcome that Americans have given the refugees serve as a reaffirmation of American awareness of the roots and ideals of our society."

## Catastrophe at the Cape

Grand Rapids native Roger B. Chaffee's dreams of soaring into space came to a sudden and tragic end during a launch pad test at Cape Kennedy on January 27, 1967, when flames suddenly filled the *Apollo 1* command module in which he and fellow astronauts Virgil "Gus" Grissom and Ed White expected to make the first manned mission of the Apollo/Saturn Program, which would eventually take men to the moon.

A review board determined that the flash fire was caused by an electrical arc following a momentary power outage, and its investigation led to design and engineering changes that made subsequent Apollo spacecraft safer.

Grissom and White were space veterans. Grissom flew a Mercury mission in 1961 and made a Gemini flight in 1965. During another 1965 Gemini mission, White became America's first spacewalker. Chaffee, who became an astronaut in 1963, had not yet ventured into space.

Another astronaut born in Grand Rapids was Jack Lousma, who joined NASA in 1966. After his birth on February 29, 1936, his family moved to the east side of the state where he graduated from Ann Arbor High School and the University of Michigan. He was the pilot of *Skylab 3* in 1973, a flight lasting fifty-nine and a half days. In 1982 he was commander of the third orbital test flight of the space shuttle *Columbia*. He spent 1,619 hours in space, 11 of them during two spacewalks.

Roger Chaffee was born in Grand Rapids on February 15, 1935, though his family's home then was in Greenville. His father, Don, was ill with the highly contagious disease of scarlet fever at the time and was quarantined. To protect others at the hospital in Greenville, his mother, Blanche, was not permitted to deliver her baby there. To avoid possible infection of herself and her two-year-old daughter, Donna, the two moved to the Grand Rapids home of Blanche's parents.

Don Chaffee, who at one time was a barnstorming pilot, introduced Roger and the rest of the family to flying in 1942 when he took them on a short excursion to Lake Michigan. Roger's interest in aviation increased during the following days as he and his father assembled model planes on a card table in the family's living room.

Also in 1942, the Chaffee family moved to Grand Rapids. After Roger's graduation from Central High School in 1953, he spent a year at the Illinois Institute of Technology in Chicago before deciding to pursue a degree in aeronautical engineering at Purdue University.

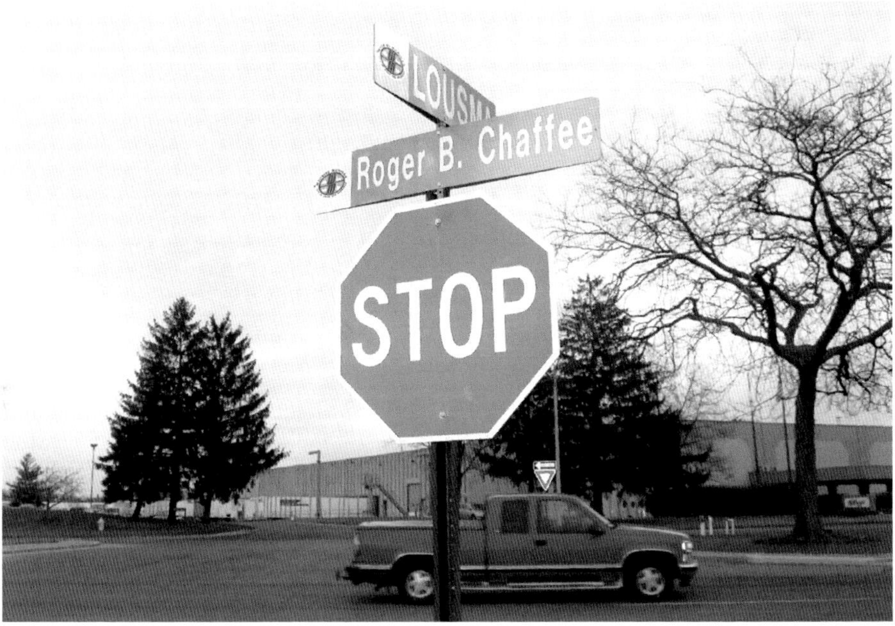


Streets in a south side industrial park that once was the Kent County Airport honor astronauts Roger Chaffee and Jack Lousma, both natives of Grand Rapids. Before he could make it into space, Chaffee died when flames erupted during a test of the *Apollo 1* module in 1967. Lousma piloted *Skylab 3* for fifty-nine and a half days in 1973 and nine years later was commander of the third orbital test flight of space shuttle *Columbia*. *Author's collection.*

At the beginning of his junior year at Purdue in 1955, he met Martha Horn on a blind date. His first opinion of the attractive young lady from Oklahoma City was that she was a naïve southern girl. She considered him a smart-aleck upperclassman. Nevertheless, he proposed to her a year later, and she accepted.

In 1957, he began flight training as a Naval Reserve Officers Training Corps air cadet and had earned his pilot's license by May. In June, he received his BS degree in aeronautical engineering from Purdue. He completed his naval training on August 22 of that year and, two days later, was in Oklahoma for his marriage to Martha.

In mid-1962, he was among 1,800 applicants for a position in the National Aviation and Space Administration's astronaut corps. Later that year, he accepted an invitation to study at the Air Force Institute of Technology at Wright-Patterson Air Force Base in Dayton, Ohio. On October 18, 1963, when he returned from a hunting trip in Michigan, he learned of his acceptance by NASA.

Christmas 1966, just one month before the tragedy at Cape Kennedy, was an especially happy one for the Chaffee family. Roger's rooftop display of Santa and his reindeer won first place in the Nassau Bay Garden Club's contest for the most beautifully decorated home. His gift to Martha was a pin that the three Apollo astronauts had designed and planned to take on their mission. However, they decided to give them at Christmas instead.

To take with them on the anticipated flight, they designed gold charms that were tiny miniatures of an Apollo module with a diamond placed at the astronaut's position in the craft. Those were to have been given to their wives when they returned.

# Index

## A



## B

**C**



**D**



**E**



**F**

**J**



**K**



**L**



**M**

**N**



**O**



**P**

## T



## U



## V



## W



## Z

# About the Author

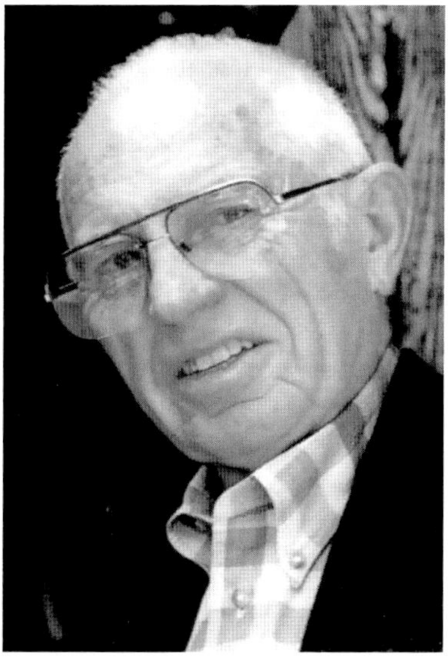

Gordon Beld began his writing career at age sixteen as a sports writer for the *Grand Rapids Press*. Today, in his mid-eighties, he is a frequent contributor to *Michigan History* and *Grand Rapids* magazines. During most of the years that he wrote and edited for the *Press* and the *Grand Rapids Herald*, he was a teacher of both history and English in suburban Grand Rapids schools. For twenty-four years he was director of news services and publications at Alma College, where his publications received several awards for excellence from national public relations associations. He was the first chairman of the Historical and Cultural Commission of the City of Wyoming, a Grand Rapids suburb. Later he was a member of the board of trustees of the Holland Area Historical Society. He has written nearly three hundred features on local and regional history for magazines and newspapers, and he is the author of a historical novel, *A Gentle Breeze from Gossamer Wings*. He holds degrees from Hope College and the University of Michigan.